TEDBooks

Why We Work

BARRY SCHWARTZ

TED Books

Simon & Schuster

London   New York   Toronto   Sydney   New Delhi

 **TED**Books

First published in Great Britain by Simon & Schuster UK Ltd, 2015
A CBS COMPANY

Copyright © 2015 by Barry Schwartz

This book is copyright under the Berne Convention.
No reproduction without permission.
All rights reserved.

The right of Barry Schwartz to be identified as the author
of this work has been asserted by him in accordance with sections
77 and 78 of the Copyright, Designs and Patents Act, 1988.

First TED Books hardcover edition September 2015

TED BOOKS and colophon are registered trademarks of
TED conferences, LLC.

For more information on licensing the TED talk that accompanies
this book, or other content partnerships with TED, please contact
TEDBooks@TED.com

3 5 7 9 10 8 6 4 2

Simon & Schuster UK Ltd
1st Floor
222 Gray's Inn Road
London WC1X 8HB

www.simonandschuster.co.uk

Simon & Schuster Australia, Sydney
Simon & Schuster India, New Delhi

A CIP catalogue record for this book is available
from the British Library

Hardback ISBN: 978-1-47114-181-2
Ebook ISBN: 978-1-47114-182-9

Interior design by MGMT.design
Jacket design by Lewis Csizmazia

Printed and bound by CPI Group (UK) Ltd, Croydon, CR0 4YY

To Ruby, Eliza, Louis, and Nico.
May your lives be full of opportunities for good work.

TABLE OF CONTENTS

The ideas of economists and political philosophers, both when they are right and when they are wrong, are more powerful than is commonly understood. Indeed the world is ruled by little else. Practical men, who believe themselves to be quite exempt from any intellectual influences, are usually the slaves of some defunct economist.

John Maynard Keynes

Why We Work

The Crucial Question

Why do we work? Why do we drag ourselves out of bed every morning instead of living lives composed of one pleasure-filled adventure after another? What a silly question. We work because we have to make a living. Sure, but is that it? Of course not. When you ask people who are fulfilled by their work why they do the work they do, money almost never comes up. The list of nonmonetary reasons people give for doing their work is long and compelling.

Satisfied workers are engaged by their work. They lose themselves in it. Not all the time, of course, but often enough for that to be salient to them. Satisfied workers are challenged by their work. It forces them to stretch themselves—to go outside their comfort zones. These lucky people think the work they do is fun, often in the way that doing crossword puzzles or Sudoku is fun.

Why else do people work? Satisfied people do their work because they feel that they are in charge. Their workday offers them a measure of autonomy and discretion. And they use that autonomy and discretion to achieve a level of mastery or expertise. They learn new things, developing both as workers and as people.

These people do their work because it's an opportunity for social engagement. They do many of their tasks as part of teams, and even when they're working alone, there are plenty of opportunities for social interaction during work's quiet moments.

Finally, these people are satisfied with their work because they find what they do meaningful. Potentially, their work makes a difference to the world. It makes other people's lives better. And it may even make other people's lives better in ways that are significant.

Of course, few occupations have all these features, and none, I suspect, have all these features all the time. But features of work like these are what get us out of the house, get us to bring work home with us, encourage us to talk about our work with others, and make us reluctant to retire. We wouldn't work if we didn't get paid, but that's not at the core of why we do what we do. And in general, we think that material rewards are a pretty bad reason for working. Indeed, when we say of someone that "he's in it for the money," we are not merely being descriptive; we're passing judgment.

These diverse sources of satisfaction from work raise some very big questions. Why is it that for the overwhelming majority of people in the world, work has few or none of these attributes? Why is it that for most of us, work is monotonous, meaningless, and soul deadening? Why is it that as capitalism developed, it created a model for work in which opportunities for the nonmaterial satisfactions that might come from it—and inspire better work—were reduced or eliminated? Workers who do *this* kind of work—whether in factories, fast-food restaurants, order-fulfillment warehouses, or indeed, in law firms, classrooms, clinics, and offices—do it for pay. Try as they might to find meaning, challenge, and room for autonomy, their work situation defeats them. The way their work is structured means that there really is little reason to do these jobs except for pay.

According to a massive report published in 2013 by Gallup, the Washington, D.C.-based polling organization, there are twice as many "actively disengaged" workers in the world as there are "engaged" workers who like their jobs. Gallup has been measuring international employee satisfaction for almost two decades. In total it has polled 25 million employees in 189 different countries. The latest version gathered information from 230,000 full-time and part-time workers in 142 countries. Overall, Gallup found that only 13 percent of workers feel engaged by their jobs. These people feel a sense of passion for their work and they spend their days helping to move their organizations forward. The vast majority of us, some 63 percent, are not engaged. We are checked out, sleepwalking through our days, putting little energy into our work. And the rest of us are actively disengaged, actually *hating* our jobs. In other words, work is more often a source of frustration than one of fulfillment for nearly 90 percent of the world's workers. Think of the social, emotional, and perhaps even economic waste that this statistic represents. Ninety percent of adults spend half their waking lives doing things they would rather not be doing at places they would rather not be.

The questions Gallup asks capture many of the reasons for work I just listed. The opportunity to do our work "right," to do our best, to be encouraged to develop and learn, to feel appreciated by coworkers and supervisors, to feel that our opinions count, to feel that what we do is important, and to have good friends at work are all aspects of work that the survey taps. And for the overwhelming majority of people, work falls short—very short. The question is why? This book will offer an answer.

1 The False Rationale

For more than two centuries, we have absorbed, as a society and as individuals, some false ideas about our relationship to work. It is a long-accepted tenet of economics, buttressed by some theories from psychology, that if you want to get someone—an employee, a student, a government official, your own child—to do something, you have to make it worth his or her while. People do things for incentives, for rewards, for money. You can see this view operating in the "carrot and stick" approach that has dominated efforts to solve the world's recent financial crisis. To prevent a financial meltdown from happening again, people argued, we needed to replace the "dumb" incentives that led to it with "smarter" ones. We had to get incentives right. Nothing else really mattered. This idea animated the inventor of the free market, <u>Adam Smith</u>. In <u>*The Wealth of Nations*,</u> published in <u>1776</u>, he wrote that:

> It is in the inherent interest of every man to live as much at his ease as he can; and if his emoluments are to be precisely the same whether he does or does not perform some very laborious duty, to perform it in as careless and slovenly a manner that authority will permit.

In other words, people work for pay—nothing more and nothing less. Smith's belief in the power of incentives led him to argue for organizing work by dividing labor into simple, easily repeated, essentially meaningless units. As long as people were getting paid for what they did, it didn't matter very much what their jobs entailed. And by dividing labor into little bits, society would gain enormous productive efficiency. In extolling the virtues of the division of labor, Smith offered a description of a pin factory that has become famous:

> One man draws out the wire, another straits it, a third cuts it, a fourth points it, a fifth grinds it at the top for receiving the head . . . I have seen a small manufactory of this kind where ten men only were employed. . . . They could make among them up-wards of forty-eight thousand pins a day. . . . But if they had all wrought separately and independently . . . they certainly could not, each of them, make twenty.

As we will see later, Smith's view of human beings was far more subtle, complex, and nuanced than what is captured in the quotes above. He did not believe that "man at work" told the full story, or even the most important story, about human nature. But in the hands of Smith's descendants, much of the nuance and subtlety was lost. More than a century later, Smith's views about work guided the father of what came to be called the "scientific management" movement, Frederick Winslow Taylor. Taylor used meticulous time and motion studies to refine the factory, as envisioned by Smith, so that human laborers were part of a well-oiled machine. And he designed compensation schemes that pushed employees to work hard, work fast, and work accurately.

Not long after that, Smith's view was echoed in the thinking of the major figure in the psychology of the mid-twentieth century, B. F. Skinner. Skinner's studies of rats and pigeons engaged in simple, repetitive tasks, over and over again, for rewards of food or water, provided the mantle of scientific rigor and a theoretical rationale for the workplace innovations developed by Taylor. Skinner showed that the behavior of animals could be powerfully influenced and precisely controlled by manipulating the amount and frequency of the rewards the behavior produced. Just as Taylor found that piecework (a fixed payment for each task completed) produced high performance in the factory, Skinner found that the pigeon equivalent of piecework produced high performance in the laboratory.

You might ask why anyone would choose to work in Smith's pin factory, putting heads on pins, minute after minute, hour after hour, day after day. Smith's answer was that, of course, people wouldn't enjoy working in the pin factory. But they wouldn't enjoy working anywhere. What Smith was telling us is that the only reason people do any kind of work is for the payoffs it produces. And as long as it produces adequate payoffs, what the work itself consists of doesn't matter.

Adam Smith was mistaken about our attitudes and aspirations regarding work. But as capitalism developed in his shadow, under the sway of the "incentive theory of everything," a mode of work evolved in which all the other satisfactions that might come from it were neglected or eliminated. And so it came to be that all over the planet, people trudged off to work each day with little expectation of meaning, engagement, or challenge. Because there was no reason to work except for the paycheck, they worked for the paycheck. So it came to be that Smith's mistaken idea about why people work became true.

I don't mean to suggest here that work was bliss prior to the industrial revolution. By no means. But the work of farmers, craftsmen, and shopkeepers, hard though it may have been, offered people a fair amount of discretion, autonomy, and variety in what they did each day. It gave them a chance to use their ingenuity to solve problems as they arose and to develop more effective ways to get their work done. All that opportunity was left behind when people walked through the factory doors.

Making False Ideas True

You might agree with Smith. You might believe that for most people, by their very natures, work is about pay and nothing more. Only the "elite" want challenge, meaning, and engagement, and can expect it from their work. Aside from being more than a little arrogant, this view is incorrect. Many people who do what we think of as mundane jobs—janitors, factory workers, call-center employees—care about more than the wage. And plenty of professionals work just for the money. What people come to seek in work largely depends on what their work makes available. And the conditions of human labor created by the industrial revolution, and perpetuated thanks in part to theories from the social sciences, have systematically deprived people of fulfillment from their work. In doing so, they have deprived people of an important source of satisfaction—and produced inferior workers in the bargain.

The lesson here is that just how important material incentives are to people will depend on how the human workplace is structured. And if we structure it in keeping with the false idea that people work only for pay, we'll create workplaces that make this false idea true. Thus, it's not true that "you just can't get good help anymore." It *is* true that you just can't get good help anymore when you only give people work to do that is deadening and soulless. What it takes to "get good help" is jobs that people want to do. And we'll see that this aspiration for good work is not "pie-in-the-sky" idealism. It is well within our grasp.

It should be said that over the years, management theory and practice have gone through periods in which the diverse motives people bring to the workplace have been acknowledged—even celebrated—and managers have been encouraged to structure the work lives of their employees so that engagement and meaning in work are possible, both for the good of the employee and for the good of the organization. Douglas McGregor's "Theory Y" was an especially influential effort along these lines a half century ago, and Stephen Barley and Gideon Kunda published an important article documenting how such ideas about management have waxed and waned over the years. But somehow, ideas like these have never stuck. The unorthodox, attention-grabbing practices of Google and other high-flying Silicon Valley companies may give the impression that assembly-line drudgery is a thing of the past. But like gravitational force, the notion that people work only for pay has repeatedly brought loftier hopes about what is possible in the workplace back down to earth. Over the centuries, Adam Smith's ideas about human nature have proven extremely resilient indeed.

Ideas or theories about human nature have a unique place in the sciences. We don't have to worry that the cosmos will be changed by our theories about the cosmos. The planets really don't care what we think or how we theorize about them. But we do have to worry that human nature will be changed by our theories of human nature. Forty years ago, the distinguished anthropologist Clifford Geertz said that human beings are "unfinished animals." What he meant is that it is human nature to have a human nature that is very much the product of the society that surrounds us. *That* human nature is more created than discovered. We "design" human nature, by designing the institutions within which people live. So we must ask ourselves just what kind of a human nature we want to help design.

If we want to help design a human nature that seeks and finds challenge, engagement, meaning, and satisfaction from work, we have to start building our way out of a deep hole that almost three centuries of misconceptions about human motivation and human nature have put us in, and help foster workplaces in which challenge, engagement, meaning, and satisfaction are possible.

2 When Work Is Good

Confronted with evidence that so few people in the world get satisfaction from their work, we need to ask why. Two ready explanations come to mind. First, many of us believe that only certain kinds of jobs permit people to find meaning, engagement, discretion, and autonomy, and opportunities to learn and grow. If we take this view, good work is just going to be the province of the few—lawyers, doctors, bankers, teachers, software developers, company CEOs, and so on. For everyone else, work will be about the paycheck. It's just the way things are. Us and them.

Alternatively, we might take the view that pretty much every job has the potential to offer people satisfying work. What stands in the way is the incredible efficiency associated with routinized, assembly-line type work. Assembly-line work can be done by people with low skill and little training, and it is responsible for the explosive economic growth we have witnessed since the beginning of the industrial revolution. Unsatisfying work is just the price people pay for a society in which affordable cars, cable TV, cell phones, and computers are the norm. Adam Smith certainly articulated this view when he talked about the growth of productivity that accompanied the division of labor in the pin factory.

So either satisfying work is not for everybody, or unsatisfying work is the price we pay for material prosperity, or both. Both of these answers to the "why" question are plausible. But both of these answers are wrong.

Cleaning Hospitals

Luke works as a custodian in a major teaching hospital. In an interview with researcher Amy Wrzesniewski and her collaborators, who were studying how people structure their work, Luke reported an incident in which he cleaned a comatose young patient's room—twice. He had already done it once, but the patient's father, who had been keeping a vigil for months, hadn't seen Luke clean the room and had snapped at him. So Luke cleaned it again. Graciously. Why? Luke explained it like this:

> Luke: I kind of knew the situation about his son. His son had been here for a long time and . . . from what I hear, his son had got into a fight and he was paralyzed. That's why he got there, and he was in a coma and he wasn't coming out of the coma. . . Well . . . I went and cleaned his room. His father would stay here every day, all day, but he smoked cigarettes. So, he had went out to smoke a cigarette and after I cleaned the room, he came back up to the room. I ran into him in the hall, and he just freaked out . . . telling me I didn't do it. I didn't clean the room and all this stuff. And at first, I got on the defensive, and I was going to argue with him. But I don't know. Something caught me and I said, "I'm sorry. I'll go clean the room."
>
> Interviewer: And you cleaned it again?
>
> Luke: Yeah, I cleaned it so that he could see me clean it . . . I can understand how he could be. It was like six months that

his son was here. He'd be a little frustrated, and so I cleaned it again. But I wasn't angry with him. I guess I could understand.

Nothing about this interaction is built into Luke's work as a custodian. Look at his job description:

- Operate carpet shampooing and upholstery cleaning equipment
- Operate mechanical cleaning and scrubbing equipment
- Strip and wax floor surfaces
- Maintain entrance area by performing such duties as sweeping, salting, and shoveling
- Clean grounds and area by performing such duties as picking up paper or trash
- Unplug commodes, urinals, and sink drains without dismantling the fixture
- Wet mop floors and stairways
- Collect and dispose of soiled linen
- Operate vacuum cleaning equipment
- Clean and wax furniture, cases, fixtures, and furnishings
- Clean mirrors, interior side of exterior glass, and both sides of interior glass
- Clean toilet rooms and fixtures
- Stock restroom supplies
- Dust venetian blinds while standing on floor or stool
- Clean patient bedside equipment
- Make beds and change linen
- Collect and transport waste materials to central location

- Wet mop small areas of floor or stairs to clean up such items as spilled liquid or food
- Replace burned-out incandescent lightbulbs
- Move and arrange furniture and furnishings
- Collect and transport soiled linen to central location

Luke's job description says nothing about responsibility or care for patients and their families. He has a long list of duties, but not a single item on the list even mentions interacting with another human being. From this description, Luke could be working in a shoe factory or a mortuary instead of a hospital.

If Luke were doing the job laid out by the job description, it would have been reasonable for him simply to have explained to the patient's father that he'd already cleaned the room, and perhaps to have brought in a supervisor to mediate if the father remained angry. Luke might have ignored the man and just gone about his business. He might have gotten angry himself.

But Luke was doing a different job than his official description would suggest. That's what Wrzesniewski and her colleagues found when they conducted in-depth interviews with Luke and other hospital custodians. The researchers had asked the custodians to talk about their jobs, and the custodians began to tell them stories about what they did. Luke's stories told them that his "official" duties were only one part of his *real* job, and that another central part of his job was to make the patients and their families feel comfortable, to cheer them up when they were down, to encourage them and divert them from their pain and their fear, and to give them a willing ear if they felt like talking. [Luke wanted to do something more than mere custodial work.]

What Luke sought in his work was shaped by the aims—what Aristotle would call the *telos*—of his organization. The telos of the hospital—promoting health, curing illness, relieving suffering—was embedded in Luke's approach to his job. The amazing thing Wrzesniewski and her colleagues discovered about Luke and many of his coworkers was that they understood and internalized these aims *in spite of* their official job description, not because of it. The job they were actually doing was one they had shaped for themselves in light of the *telos* of medical care. Ben, another custodian, told the researchers how he stopped mopping the hallway floor because a patient who was recovering from major surgery was out of his bed getting a little much-needed exercise by walking slowly up and down the hall. Corey told them about how he ignored his supervisor's admonitions and refrained from vac-uuming the visitors' lounge while some family members, who were there all day, every day, happened to be napping. These custodians shaped their jobs with the central purpose of the hospital in mind.

Job crafting is what Wrzesniewski and her colleagues called it. Luke, Ben, and Corey were not generic custodians; they were *hospital* custodians. They saw themselves as playing an important role in an institution whose aim is to see to the care and welfare of patients. So, when Luke was confronted by the angry father and he had to decide what to do, he could not look the answer up in his official job description because the rules that defined his job said nothing about situations like this. What guided him was the aim of the job he had crafted.

What is it that enabled Luke to do work like this? First, Luke's job gave him broad discretion when it came to social interactions with the patients. He didn't have a supervisor looking over his shoulder every minute. Further, the challenge of getting these social interactions right was engaging. Meeting the challenge demanded empathy, good listening, and the perceptiveness to know when to stay in the background and when to come forward, when to joke and when to comfort. Having the skills to do this work well made Luke's day. And it likely helped to make the patients' days better as well.

Finally, Luke believed in the purposes of the enterprise of which he was a part. A belief like this helped make his work meaningful. Yes, Luke and his colleagues were custodians. But they were custodians in a *hospital*—a place where staff struggles to cure disease and alleviate suffering, and where every day, as people go about their jobs, lives hang in the balance. As Peter Warr, a professor of work psychology, has pointed out, to be satisfied with our work, we typically need a belief in the purpose of what we do.

Amy Wrzesniewski's research systematizes the aspects of work that help people find meaning and satisfaction, even in occupations like hospital cleaning, that don't seem to lend themselves to it. She calls work that has such characteristics a "calling" and distinguishes it from work that is a "job" or a "career." People who see their work as a "job" enjoy little discretion and experience minimal engagement or meaning. People with jobs see work as a necessity of life, they work for pay, they would switch jobs if given the chance to earn more money, they can't wait to retire, and they would not encourage their friends or children to follow in their footsteps. They are the embodiment of Adam Smith's ideas about people's attitudes toward work.

People who see their work as a "career" generally enjoy more discretion and are more engaged. They may even enjoy what they do. But their focus is on advancement. They see themselves as following a trajectory that leads to promotion, higher salary, and better work.

It is people who see their work as a "calling" who find it most satisfying. For them, work is one of the most important parts of life, they are pleased to be doing it, it is a vital part of their identity, they believe their work makes the world a better place, and they would encourage their friends and children to do this kind of work. People whose work is a calling get great satisfaction from what they do.

What, then, determines how people think about their work? To some degree, it depends on characteristics of the person. That is, differences in the way people approach their work are explained by the attitudes they bring to their work—who *they* are, not what the work is. After all, not every hospital custodian is like Luke, Ben, and Corey.

But the kind of work one does is also a major factor. It is easier to find meaning and engagement in some kinds of work than in others. Take discretion, engagement, and meaning out of work and people feel less "called" to it and get less satisfaction from doing it. As they get less satisfaction from doing it, they do it less well. As they do it less well, their supervisors take even more discretion away.

Wrzesniewski's interviews with hospital custodians revealed, again and again, that their greatest source of satisfaction came from their interactions with patients. That is when they felt the most useful, the most important, the most skilled. And having staff members like Luke is a precious resource. What a gift for the patients, the hospital, and the custodians themselves that there are employees who want to be a part of the caring mission of a hospital, who are willing to learn how to do it well, and who take great satisfaction and pride in their work. "Making a patient smile can make my day," one custodian explained to Wrzesniewski.

Carlotta, a colleague of Luke's, told Wrzesniewski about her custodial work in a unit of the hospital where people recovered from various brain injuries and were often comatose for extended periods of time. Carlotta took it upon herself to change the pictures on the walls in these patients' rooms as a subtle means of cheering them up by hinting that they are making progress. As Carlotta described it: "Sometimes I'll change the pictures on the wall, like every week, 'cause our patients stay for months and months and months . . . so they know they're getting that much closer to being home." Carlotta was clear about the joy this kind of effort brought her:

> I enjoy entertaining the patients. That's what I enjoy the most.
> And that is not really part of my job description. But I like putting
> on a show for them, per se. Dancing if there is a certain song on.
> I get to dance and if a talk show is on, I get to talk about that talk

show or whatever. That's what I enjoy the most. I enjoy making the patients laugh.

But Carlotta not only knew when and how to make a patient laugh, and took joy in doing so. She also knew when care involved a strong hand and a brave heart, and this too made her work a source of satisfaction. Carlotta explained:

> One of our patients was in distress and he was a quad [quadriplegic], and I just happened to be there when he was stressing out, and so I pushed the button [for staff assistance] and I told them to get in here . . . They were drawing his blood in one arm and trying to stick an IV in the other and he wasn't into needles . . . so I stayed with him while the nurses did what they had to do because he was sliding out of his wheelchair, he was getting ready to pass out, you know, and so the nurse wanted to take his blood pressure and he wouldn't let her because he was kind of upset with them, and I explained to him, I said, "Well, listen, I'm going to give you five minutes to kind of calm down, but they have to take your blood pressure to make sure everything else is going all right, and I will stay in here with you." So that's what I did, I stayed there with him and let him calm down and I told the nurse, "Come on in and take his blood pressure." . . . From that point on I think we were buddies for life. . . . I just happened to be in the right place at the right time.

Luke and Carlotta were not actively encouraged to craft their work into callings. Meaningful and engaged work emerged because they wanted to craft their jobs into callings, and—and this is key—because it was not forbidden.

Why would anyone forbid people to work the way Luke and Carlotta work? One reason is efficiency. If custodians just put their heads down and go about ticking off the items in their job descriptions, they'll get "more" done. As a result, the hospital can employ fewer of them, and give them more rooms to clean. The hospital will save money.

A second reason is the desire on the part of managers for control. If custodians simply go about performing the items in their job description, then supervisors control what they do by controlling the job description. But if they start freelancing— deviating from their scripts to step into the breach when help is needed, then control moves from the manager to the managed. Many years ago, economist Stephen Marglin wrote an important article called "What Do Bosses Do?" in which he argued that a central and often unacknowledged consequence of the assembly-line division of labor is that it takes control of the job away from the person who is doing it and gives it to the boss— the person who constructs the assembly line.

So, in the service of efficiency and control, a manager could beat the improvisations of Luke and Carlotta out of them. Their work would be much impoverished, and the hospital would run less well, as a result.

Making Carpet

You might think it's relatively easy to find meaning and purpose in your work—regardless of the job—if you're working in a hospital that is saving lives every day. Judging from my own experience observing how invisible custodians and other "dirty workers" are to those around them, I don't think it's easy at all. But let's suppose it is. Would you say the same thing about people who work in a factory that makes carpet?

About twenty years ago, Ray Anderson, the late CEO of the immensely successful carpet manufacturer, Interface, had what he described as an epiphany. Here he was, with more money than he or his heirs would know what to do with, when he realized that his company was poisoning the environment. Carpet making is (or was) a petroleum-intensive industry and Interface's environmental footprint was huge. Anderson wondered what good it would do to leave his grandchildren great wealth if the price of accumulating that wealth was an uninhabitable planet. So Anderson resolved to transform every aspect of Interface's operations, moving to achieve a zero footprint goal by 2020. He assumed that the development of new production processes and a commitment to pollution control would cost money—a lot of it. But he was willing to sacrifice the bottom line to achieve a social good.

So Interface began a journey to change what it makes, how it makes it, and what it does with its waste. As of 2013, it had cut energy use in half, shifted to renewable energy, and cut waste to a tenth of what it was. How much profit was sacrificed? None at all! Interface employees were so motivated by the opportunity to work for the common good, and challenged by the need to find innovative modifications of the production process, that their work became much more effective and efficient. And the company, realizing that its new mission would demand creative partnership from top to bottom of the organization, flattened its hierarchy and gave employees much more discretion and control over what they did. The strength of the company's shared vision encouraged collaboration and cooperation. Progress toward sustainability required creative solutions. So a culture that encouraged openness and allowed for failure emerged. In the company's words:

> The evidence of a successful, lasting cultural change at Interface can be found in the great number of innovations conceived of and implemented by employees on the shop floor. Interface employees are connected to something bigger than making carpet. Sustainability has inspired and empowered associates with a committed sense of higher purpose.

The result of Anderson's vision, twenty years out, is a company that remains extremely successful and is populated by employees who are eager to come to work every day. He documented the transformation of Interface in his 2009 book, *Confessions of a Radical Industrialist: Profits, People, Purpose—Doing Business by Respecting the Earth*. You don't need to be working for an organization that saves lives to find meaning and purpose in what you do. You just need to be doing work that makes people's lives better.

Cutting Hair

It's true that the people who work at Interface don't save lives, but they are on a mission to save the planet. Few of us can find such a noble calling in what we do. What about people whose work is not globally impactful—restaurant servers, plumbers, roofers, welders, hairdressers, and office workers? Here, too, it is possible to find enormous meaning and satisfaction in what you do. When Amy Wrzesniewski was studying jobs, careers, and callings, one of her samples of employees was a set of administrative assistants working at a college. She found that roughly a third of them viewed their work as a calling; they were providing key logistical support for faculty who were working to shape the minds of the next generation. What could be more meaningful than that?

Mike Rose interviewed people with everyday, blue-collar jobs in *The Mind at Work*. His chapter on hairdressers is particularly eye opening. To be sure, hairdressers need to acquire a set of technical skills—for cutting, coloring, and styling hair. And many, perhaps most of them, see what they do as requiring a fair amount of creativity. But what makes the job meaningful, I think, is the skill they acquire in interacting with clients. What does a client mean when she says she wants this haircut a little "fresher"? How do you talk a client out of a haircut that looks great on the long, angular face of the model whose photo she has brought in but will look terrible on the client's pumpkin-shaped face? How do you help clients feel good about their appearance—confident as they leave the shop to face the world? The hairdressers Rose interviewed were proud of their technical skills and reveled in the complexity of such a seemingly simple act as cutting hair. But they were also proud of their ability to understand, talk to, and manage people. This was an essential part of their job. And doing it well could make a big difference to the quality of the lives of the people they served.

"It's important to *hear* my client," said one stylist. "The consultation is the most important moment of the haircut." "Don't assume you know what they want," said another stylist, "because *they* may not even know what they want." Another stylist pointed out that a client will say, "I want an inch off," then show you two inches with her fingers. Appreciative clients say things like this about their stylists: "She listens." She "respects what I want." She "sees what I mean." Stylists who love their work love its technical complexity and room for creativity. But also "I just like making people happy. . . . People leave my chair happy because of what I did for them. You really don't get that out of too many jobs, you know, that you're gonna affect people like that." Another stylist observed that "This is a business that is unlike most; there's something very nurturing about it. It is one of the few places in our society where you have permission to touch people. It's so intimate. We humans have a need for connection."

The lesson from the custodians, the carpet makers, and the hairdressers is that virtually any job has the potential to offer people satisfaction. Jobs can be organized to include variety, complexity, skill development, and growth. They can be organized to provide the people who do them with a measure of autonomy. And perhaps most important, they can be made meaningful by connecting them to the welfare of others.

This last point just can't be overemphasized. Management researcher Adam Grant and various collaborators have shown that just by making salient the potential effects of one's work

on others, a work force can be inspired. Consider this example.
Many universities employ undergraduates to reach out by phone
to alumni and parents of current students and ask for contribu-
tions. What could be more delightful than a call from your alma
mater, asking for money? Do you pick it up when caller ID tells
you who's calling? If you do, do you politely let the solicitor finish her spiel? If, by some miracle, you do, do you actually make
a contribution? These calls are annoying and nervy, after all the
money you paid in tuition. Now imagine yourself on the other
end, spending two or three hours making calls to people who
don't want to answer them, and soliciting people who don't want
to respond. It's a tough way to make a living, and the success
rate of these solicitations is minuscule. But what Grant found
is that a tiny intervention, designed to remind callers of the
purpose of their calls, was transformative. Grant arranged for
solicitors to be visited by a student who owed his life-changing
scholarship to phone solicitations just like this. The student was
effusive in his enthusiasm for his education and his gratitude to
those who made it possible.

Having heard the student, the solicitors went off to do their
excruciating jobs. Miraculously, their performance was trans-
formed. They made more calls per hour, and got many more con-
tributions, than did a comparable group of solicitors who had not
heard the student. Same job. Same pay. But inspired by seeing
the effects of their efforts vividly portrayed, twice as effective.
Such is the power of giving work meaning and significance.

Perhaps it goes without saying that doctors, lawyers, educators, and other professionals often do work they find

meaningful, significant, and fulfilling. But now we've seen that custodians, carpet factory workers, hairdressers, and phone solicitors can find an equal level of meaning and fulfillment. To have a job that you are happy—even eager—to do, it helps if the work itself is challenging, varied, and engaging. It helps if the work gives you the chance to use your skills and develop more skills. It helps if you have discretion over how you do your job. It helps if you feel that you are part of a group, with fellow workers you respect. And most important, it helps if the work is aimed at a goal that is valuable and gives the work you do meaning and purpose. The hospital custodians washed floors the same way custodians in an office building would, but with a higher purpose. The same could be said of Adam Grant's phone solicitors. Whereas good work need not have all of these positive characteristics, this last one—a sense of higher purpose—may be close to indispensable.

Though all the hospital custodians interviewed by Wrzesniewski were doing the same nominal job, not all of them were doing it like Luke or Carlotta. So it is possible that if people bring the right attitude to their work, almost any job can provide satisfaction, and if they don't bring the right attitude, no job will provide satisfaction.

There is no doubt that the attitudes people bring to their work are important, but I think there are limits to what an individual can do psychologically to interpret a soulless job as a meaningful one. Those people working in Adam Smith's pin factory would have to do quite a psychological number on themselves in order to see their work as engaging and purposeful. That said, often it doesn't take a lot to turn almost any job into an opportunity for meaning and engagement. Doing so makes work better for the workers. It also makes work better for the people they serve and for the companies that employ them.

This last fact should give you real pause. If satisfying work makes for better workers, surely market competition would have seen to it that every company organized work to enable employees to get satisfaction out of the jobs they did. If the work environment at your company was rigid, monotonous, hierarchical, and punitive, a competitor would create a less hostile workplace, nurture more productive workers, and drive your company out of business. We've been doing this market-competition thing for a long time, and you'd think that by now, conditions of work would surely have evolved to produce maximum efficiency.

If you thought that, you'd be wrong. Such is the power of the ideology about people's distaste for work that was handed down by Adam Smith and elaborated on since. Management expert Jeffrey Pfeffer laid it all out in his book *The Human Equation*. Pfeffer's book was not concerned especially with asking what it takes to create workplaces in which people thrive. He was asking what it takes to create workplaces that succeed—that make for growing, sustainably profitable companies. But based on his analysis of many companies in many different lines of business, what makes for successful companies overlaps substantially with what makes for good work. In his words, a good company nurtures "high commitment" workers, and high commitment workers care about doing their jobs well. Pfeffer identifies a number of factors that effective organizations have in common:

1. They provide a high degree of employment security, which builds employee loyalty and trust.

2. They rely on self-managed teams and decentralized decision-making. That is, employees are given a lot of discretion and autonomy. This also enhances trust, in addition to reducing the need for employees whose main job is to watch other employees.

3. They pay more than the market demands, which makes employees feel valued. But they don't rely very much on individual incentives to induce people to work hard. When the company does well, all employees benefit through some form of gain sharing. They're all in it together.

4. They provide extensive training, both when people start to work and as an ongoing process. This training represents a significant investment in employees, which again builds loyalty and trust. And continued training means that employees keep facing new challenges and developing new skills. By way of contrast, Pfeffer reports a study showing that in the automobile industry, Japan spends an average of 364 hours training each new employee, Europe spends 178, and the United States spends 21.

5. They measure employee performance, but they don't *over*measure employee performance, trusting that their employees will want to do right by the company and, with enough training, will succeed.

6. They put great emphasis on the company mission, not just in occasional speeches by the CEO, but in day-to-day practices up and down the organization.

Companies that have all or most of these characteristics are
industry leaders, across many industries. Companies that rely
on performance bonuses and other incentives, on close supervision, on minimizing individual employee responsibility and
discretion, and on saving money on training by designing jobs
that don't take much training, lag behind. And Pfeffer suggests
something of a downward spiral. A company starts to have
trouble, because of low profits, high costs, and poor customer
service. This leads to efforts to cut costs and make the company
"lean and mean": less training, salary reductions, layoffs, part-
time workers, a freeze on hiring and promotion. These changes
lead to decreased worker motivation to excel, decreased effort,
even worse customer service, less job satisfaction and more
turnover, which in turn leads to more trouble for the business.
In short, you take discretion, engagement, and meaning out of
work and people get less satisfaction from doing it. As they get
less satisfaction from doing it, they do it less well. As they do it
less well, their supervisors take even more discretion away. The
"cure" makes the disease even worse.

Turning a "Vicious Cycle" into a "Virtuous Cycle"

As Pfeffer describes it, the knee-jerk response to competitive
pressure—cutting staff, speeding up workers, monitoring
performance closely—makes the situation worse, by reducing
the effectiveness (and the satisfaction) of the workforce. Thus, it
creates a vicious cycle, as the more employers do to try to regain
their edge, the further behind they fall. By contrast, paying
attention to enhancing the character of work creates what we

might call a virtuous cycle. When people find engagement and meaning in the work they do, it makes them happy to go to work, and as psychologist Barbara Fredrickson has shown, when people are happy, they work better and they work smarter. Much of Fredrickson's work is summarized in her book *Positivity*, and her central insight is that when people are in states of positive emotion, they think expansively and creatively. They are in what Fredrickson calls a "broaden and build" mode of engagement with the world. When people are in states of negative emotion, in contrast, they hunker down defensively, worried about making mistakes or going wrong. Danger gives us tunnel vision. But when we're not under threat, and get satisfaction from the work we do, our positive emotional state will enable us to do better work, which in turn will create more positive emotion, which in turn will promote even better work, and so on. Positivity nurtures itself, and an environment is created in which the work just keeps getting better, and the workers just keep getting more satisfaction out of what they do. Everybody wins—the workers, their employers, and the clients and customers.

There is something to notice about the theory of how competitive markets work that should make us optimistic that satisfying work is within the grasp of every employee at every organization. Market theory tells us that each transaction is what is called "positive-sum." In other words, both the buyer and the seller of goods or services gains from the transaction. If I wasn't going to benefit from buying the shirt I'm considering, I wouldn't buy it. And if you weren't going to benefit from selling me the shirt, you wouldn't sell it. So in theory, every market transaction leaves both parties better off. This positive-sum structure is in contrast to, say, a poker game, in which every dollar that someone wins is a dollar that someone else loses. What this market logic means is that virtually every job that people do can be seen as improving the lives of customers, even if only in small ways. And what that means is that virtually every job that people do can be made meaningful by focusing on the ways in which it improves the lives of customers, as long as it's done right and done well.

We can see the virtuous cycle played out in the story of Market Basket, a grocery chain with stores scattered throughout New England. In 1917, two Greek immigrants, Athanasios and Efrosini Demoulas, opened a small grocery store in Lowell, Massachusetts. Over time, the one small store grew to many large ones, spreading throughout New England, and leadership was passed down to the next generation. Though the business continued to grow and prosper, there was almost continuous acrimony among the family members who owned and ran it. Law suits proliferated, fights for control escalated, and accusations of sabotage flew. Control eventually devolved into the hands of two cousins, Arthur S. and Arthur T. Demoulas. Though Arthur T. was president of the company, Arthur S. controlled a slight majority of the stock, and the conflict continued. But through it all, the supermarket chain continued to thrive. Market Basket now has more than seventy stores and employs more than twenty thousand people.

By almost all accounts, Arthur T. ran the business as if it were still an intimate, family operation. Employees were paid well and participated in profit sharing. But perhaps more important, Arthur T. took an interest in them personally, knowing many employees by name, and making sure he was familiar with their family circumstances. He and his employees, in turn, treated the customers as family, keeping prices low and products wholesome and high quality. Market Basket even lowered its prices by 4 percent, across the board, in response to the economic downturn that followed the financial collapse of 2008 and had devastated the lives of many customers. "Our customers need the money more than we do," Arthur T. said. Market Basket employees worked with dedication, enthusiasm, and a spirit of cooperation, committed to the views that their own work was important and respected, and that they were performing a vital community function.

But all was not well. The family feud continued and in June of 2014 Arthur T. was fired. And then something amazing happened. Many employees responded by refusing to go to work. They did this at the risk of losing their jobs, at a time when no one could take having a job for granted. And customers joined in, refusing to continue shopping at the store. Here were many thousands of working-class people rising up in support of a billionaire. The shelves grew emptier and emptier. The stores became virtual ghost towns. This went on for two months, imperiling the future of the company. Finally, at the end of August 2014, Arthur T. agreed to buy out his rival relatives and was restored as president. After much celebration, employees went back to work, food went back on the shelves, and customers went back to the aisles.

"We keep it as simple as possible for people," Arthur T. said in an interview. "We keep costs low and quality high. We keep the stores clean and offer service with a smile. And if at the end of the day you have some success, then you share that with the associates." Asked to explain the broad support he got from customers and employees alike, Arthur T. said that, "I think so many people could relate to it because it affects everyone. If everyone in the workplace is equal and treated with dignity, they work with a little extra passion, a little extra dedication. I think that's a wonderful business message to the world."

Why do we find stories like this so inspiring? They inspire us because they surprise us. We simply don't expect to find this kind of dedication and commitment from employees who do checkout, bagging, shelf-stocking, product delivery, or deli service—even when we are those workers, ourselves—nor do we expect the people who own supermarkets to prioritize anything but the bottom line. We don't expect this kind of empathy in the workplace. Yet, at Market Basket, it's there. Why? And why is it that so few of us have stories like this to tell about our own work?

In It for the Money

In Jeffrey Pfeffer's telling, supported by the Gallup survey on work satisfaction, the striking thing about good management practices is how rare they are. We may not expect business leaders to ask themselves "How can I make my employees' lives better by restructuring their jobs?" But we surely would expect them to ask themselves "How can I make my business better by restructuring employees' jobs?" As Adam Smith famously imagined in describing the "invisible hand" of market competition, when markets are competitive, we don't need good intentions to improve human welfare; competition among selfish individuals does it for us. If competition will improve the lives of consumers of goods and services, as no doubt it has, surely it should also improve the lives of *producers* of goods and services as well. Good practices should drive out the bad. To some degree, in some occupations, this has happened. Managers have slowly come to realize that the organization benefits from enabling people to do work that they actually want to do. But it hasn't penetrated very deeply into the bowels of organizations. For the educated elite, work isn't just about money. But for the rank and file, what else is there but money? Recall Adam Smith:

> It is in the inherent interest of every man to live as much at his ease as he can; and if his emoluments are to be precisely the same whether he does or does not perform some very laborious duty, to perform it in as careless and slovenly a manner that authority will permit.

If you are a business owner who believes Smith's account of the rank and file, then you design a system to manage them based on this belief. Such a system will rely on wages to motivate, and highly monitored, simplified routine, so that laziness and inattention won't have disastrous consequences. And in such a system, Adam Smith will be right. Why else would someone show up at the pin factory every day except for the wage?

The two standard methods for managing disinterested workers are material incentives (wages) and close monitoring of work that has been routinized. Carrots and sticks. What is striking is that, in the analysis that Pfeffer offers, *both* of these tools have negative effects on employee engagement and work satisfaction. Nonetheless, they are the first tools that employers reach for. This not only prevents custodians and assembly-line workers from having good work, but as it trickles up to higher and higher levels of the organization, it can warp almost any work into bad work.

3 How Good Work Goes Bad: Rules and Incentives over Integrity

Toward the end of high school and early in college, I had a series of summer jobs that taught me a lot about what most work is like. One summer I worked in a clothing factory. My job was to take garments that had been readied for pressing and bring them to the pressers. These men (they were all men) spent eight hours a day, every day, performing the same operations, over and over again. The factory heat was intense (no air-conditioning), but around the pressing machines it was close to unbearable. And the pressers were being paid by the piece, so that the faster they worked, the more they earned. And they worked plenty fast. The lesson I learned from watching these men toil was simple: Stay in school.

After several weeks of this work, I was shifted to a different job, bringing finished garments to a group of women (they were all women) for final inspection before the garments left the factory. Work was a little less unpleasant for the inspectors than for the pressers. They were sitting rather than standing. They were not near the pressing-machine infernos. And they got paid by the hour. As a result, the pace of their work was a little more relaxed, and they passed the time chatting and gossiping with one another as they inspected the clothing. They barely paid attention to what they were doing. Like the pressers, the inspectors did the same thing over and over again. But they managed to make their work automatic enough that their minds could be otherwise engaged. Stay in school.

The next summer, I worked in an air-conditioned office, filing financial reports. There were a half-dozen other young men (we were all men) doing just what I was doing. The work was mind numbing. Eight hours felt like a week. And we all had to look as though our minds were on our work because we worked in the center of a very large room, surrounded by the cubicles of our superiors, any one of whom might be scrutinizing us at any moment. Stay in school!

The summer after that I was again in a factory, working in the shipping department. Picking clothes off racks, putting them into boxes, and sealing and addressing the boxes was hardly a step up from my previous jobs. But I loved it. I loved it because I was busy. But more important, I loved it because this particular factory was owned by my family (a very small manufacturer of women's clothing) and for that reason, I felt deeply engaged in contributing to the family business. I watched what was going on around me, thought about ways we might make various parts of the production process work more efficiently, and asked lots of questions. By the end of the summer, I felt that I understood how my family made its living. I can't honestly say that I thought deeply about how what I was doing might be meaningful and improve the lives of others, but, like the workers at Interface, feeling like I was a key part of a worthwhile enterprise was enough to make me look forward to going to work, and to doing good work myself.

I got one more lesson about what work can be in the next summer, when I worked as a research assistant in a laboratory.

The research being done involved experiments on how rewards and punishments controlled the behavior of rats and pigeons. Though I didn't realize it at the time, this work provided the conceptual underpinning for what I had observed in the clothing factory three years before.

The thing about this job was that the work I actually did could not have been more routine and menial. Take animals out of their cages and transport them to the setting in which the experiment was being done. Push a button to start the experiment. Come back an hour later to record the data, take the animal back to its cage, and repeat the procedure with the next animal. Eight hours a day of pretty unskilled activity. But for me it was thrilling. I was being a scientist. I understood why the experiments were being done, and how they might contribute to our understanding of behavior. Though it was not an official part of my job, I read reports of previous experiments, done by others, that might bear on what we were doing. I thought about what we might discover next, based on the results of the current experiment. And I participated in meetings with all the people working in the lab—my professor, graduate students, and undergraduates like me. This, too, was not part of my job, but doing it eagerly made my official job much more meaningful to me.

So on my path to adulthood, I did some bad work and I did some good work. And the difference between the good and the bad had less to do with my actual duties than it did with the context in which my duties were embedded. Someone working beside me, either in my family's business or in the psychology lab, might have regarded what she did as just a job, or even a bad job. But not me. There was meaning to be found in those activities, and I was able to find it. The lesson I draw—half a century later—from my varied summer work experiences is that it needn't take a lot to turn bad work into good. And it needn't take a lot to turn good work into bad. Here, we'll investigate how we can turn good work into bad work, largely as a result of the mistaken assumption that the people who are working don't want to be there, and thus have to be carefully monitored and incentivized to do their work.

Think about Adam Smith's pin factory. In the name of efficiency, his vision was to divide tasks up into simple, easily repeated operations—operations that took almost no training or skill. You could have someone working productively on the assembly line in no time. And given Smith's assumptions about human nature, the gain in efficiency was accomplished at no cost. People were lazy by nature and despised work, so by giving them this kind of monotonous work to do, the manager was taking nothing away from them. Pay is what would motivate them to work accurately and quickly.

Henry Ford, of course, created the most famous descendant of Smith's model, and there is no doubt that it was efficient. The Ford assembly line brought the price of automobiles within the reach of ordinary people. Over the years, the efficiency of factories only grew, as F. W. Taylor, in his book *The Principles of Scientific Management*, laid out in microscopic detail the best ways to divide production into individual jobs, so that little skill or attention was required, and the best way to arrange pay, so that maximum effort would be produced.

Factories like this have mostly left American shores, but one sees the same pattern played out in modern versions of the factory, like call centers and order-fulfillment centers. Workers in both environments are micromanaged. In call centers, they're given detailed scripts to follow (which is necessary, since they are often located in a different country, thousands of miles away, have trouble with the language and, beyond the scripts, know almost nothing of the products or services about which they are taking calls). Is this an efficient way for human beings to spend their time? That depends on how you do the accounting. When people have this kind of work to do, they are deprived of the meaning and engagement we encountered in the last chapter. So every worker spends half of his or her waking life deprived. Perhaps the pay compensates, but I don't think so. And existing research bears me out. In a comprehensive article about the significance of salary to job satisfaction, Timothy Judge and colleagues reviewed the results of eighty-six studies that included about fifteen thousand employees. Their analysis of the data from all these studies combined suggested that level of pay had very little effect on either job satisfaction or pay satisfaction.

So it is unlikely that pay compensates for routinized, meaningless work. More likely, such workers are resigned to living lives in which their work is nothing but drudgery.

The role of assumptions about human nature in maintaining these kinds of workplaces is striking. As Jeffrey Pfeffer detailed in _The Human Equation_, we have thirty years of evidence that organizing work differently not only gives the workers the opportunity to get some satisfaction out of what they do, it also enhances the company's bottom line. In what has become a famous example of the benefits of organizing production in a way that engages employees, Toyota, whose system of production gives workers a great deal more autonomy and variety in what they do than a typical assembly line, took over a failed General Motors plant in California in 1983. They didn't change the workforce. They didn't change the equipment. All they changed was the production system. The result was a dramatic improvement in both productivity and quality. When you create an environment in which workers are respected, they want to be there and they want to work. The labor costs associated with the production of vehicles dropped almost 50 percent under the Toyota production system.

There is little reason to believe that we as a society have learned Toyota's lesson. Indeed, we seem to have moved in the opposite direction, turning jobs that demand judgment, flexibility, challenge, and engagement into the white-collar equivalent of factory work. Consider education. There is much hand wringing about the failures of American education, which seem to be pervasive. And there seems to be broad agreement that the single biggest factor in determining how much children learn is the quality of the teachers. So what have we done to improve the quality of American schoolteachers? In large part, what we've done is create systems that are designed to make teacher quality irrelevant. Curriculum specialists, sitting in offices at boards of education, design curricula that are "idiot proof," spelling out in excruciating detail how the lessons should go.

The idea, borrowed from Adam Smith, Henry Ford, and F. W. Taylor, is that if you create a smart system, you don't need smart and dedicated teachers. My colleague Ken Sharpe and I documented some examples of rule- and script-driven education a few years ago in our book *Practical Wisdom*. For example, consider Christine Jabbari, a kindergarten teacher in Chicago. On day fifty-three of the school year, Ms. Jabbari joined all the other kindergarten teachers in the Chicago system in teaching the letter *B* to her students. The binder she used identified the section of the Iowa Test of Basic Skills to which that day's lesson plan corresponded, and provided step-by-step questions and conversation starters.

> Script for Day: 053
> TITLE: Reading and enjoying literature/words with "b"
> TEXT: *The Bath*
> LECTURE: Assemble students on the rug or reading area. . . . Give students a warning about the dangers of hot water. . . . Say, "Listen very quietly as I read the story." . . . Say, "Think of other pictures that make the same sound as the sound bath begins with."

The script Jabbari followed was twice as long as the book she was reading.

Or consider Donna Moffett, who taught first grade at a public school in Brooklyn. At forty-six, full of idealism and enthusiasm, she abandoned her $60,000-a-year job as a legal secretary to earn $37,000 teaching in one of New York's most troubled schools. When she began her "literacy block" at 11:58 one Wednesday in May, she opened the textbook to Section 1, "Pets Are Special Animals." Her mentor, veteran teacher Marie Buchanan, was sitting in. When Ms. Moffett got to a line about a boy mischievously drawing on a table, she playfully noted, "Just like some students in here." Mrs. Buchanan frowned. "You don't have to say that." When Ms. Moffett turned to a page that suggested an art project related to the story and started passing out paper, Mrs. Buchanan commented: "You're not going to have time to complete that." After the lesson, Mrs. Buchanan pulled her aside. "You have to prepare for these lessons and closely follow your teacher's guide. We're going to do this again tomorrow, and you're not going to wing it."

The teacher's manual Ms. Moffett was using (which included an actual script and specified the time to spend on each activity, from thirty seconds to forty minutes) was also being used in hundreds of schools nationwide. The manual's fixed routines and careful instructions are sometimes helpful to novice teachers; they can act as training wheels on a bicycle, enabling them to keep their balance when they first start teaching in the chaotic environment of an inner-city public school. But this is not what Ms. Moffett thought she was signing up for when she switched careers. When she applied to the teaching program in New York, she wrote: "I want to manage a classroom where children experience the thrill of wonder, the joy of creativity, and the rewards of working hard. My objective is to convey to children in their formative years the sheer pleasure in learning." But that's not what she got.

The New York Board of Education required teachers in low-performing schools to follow a rigid curriculum, as has become common in many school systems. In some systems, teachers' annual evaluations, and even pay, are based on their students' performance on standardized tests, and the scripted curricula are written to prepare students to pass these tests. In other systems, the kind of micromonitoring of teacher behavior that Mrs. Buchanan was doing as a temporary mentor is permanently built into the system. School administrators observe teachers, armed with a generic checklist applicable to all subjects, all grade levels, all children, and all teachers. An hour's teaching is broken down into several dozen observable, measurable behaviors. You can see the influence of F. W. Taylor in all these efforts at school reform.

Standardized scripted curricula are tied directly to standardized tests, which are the most common measure of educational progress. These tests are high stakes, in that schools and teachers are rewarded (more money) or punished (funds denied, schools closed, staff dismissed or reassigned) based on student test performance. Most states have such systems, and the No Child Left Behind Act of 2001 required all states to administer standardized reading and math tests in third and eighth grade. School systems risk losing federal funding if students consistently fail to meet the standards. Standardized tests gave birth to standardized, scripted curricula. If schools and teachers would be rated, funded, and paid based on student test performance, it made sense to mandate that teachers use materials explicitly designed so that students could pass the tests.

Supporters of this approach to education were not out to undermine the engagement, creativity, and energy of good teachers. The scripted curricula and tests were aimed at improving the performance of weak teachers in failing schools—or forcing them out of teaching altogether. If lesson plans were tied to tests, teachers' scripts would tell them what to do to get the students ready. All teachers, novice or expert, weak or strong, would be required to follow the standardized system.

Teachers on the front lines often complain about what is left out of the teach-to-test paradigm, pointing out that at best, these tests are only one indicator of student learning. One of the chief criticisms many teachers make is that the system is dumbing down their teaching. It is de-skilling them. It is not allowing them to use their judgment, nor is it helping them to develop the judgment they need to teach well. They are encouraged, says education scholar Linda Darling-Hammond, "to present material that [is] beyond the grasp of some and below the grasp of others, to sacrifice students' internal motivations and interests in the cause of 'covering the curriculum,' and to forgo the *teachable moment*, when students [are] ready and eager to learn, because it [happens] to fall outside of the prescribed sequence of activities." Sooner or later, turning out kids who can turn out the right answers the way you turn out screws, or hubcaps, or pins, comes to seem like normal practice.

Virtually all of the practices that we've learned lead to good work are violated by the reliance on detailed scripts to produce assembly-line education. It is the very antithesis of smart job design. Over time, it is sure to produce the antithesis of smart performance. And the most tragic consequence of this de-skilling is that it will either drive the energy, engagement, and enthusiasm out of good teachers, or it will drive these good teachers out of education.

But there is another aspect of many modern work settings that may be even more destructive to good work than routinization and excessive supervision. That is the reliance on material incentives as the principal motivator of employees. Carefully crafted incentive schemes, designed to ensure top performance, can often produce the opposite—competition among employees, and efforts to game the system and look good on whatever metric is being used to assign pay and bonuses without actually producing the underlying results that the metric is meant to assess. The standardized tests that accompanied teachers' scripts were an attempt to produce a metric on which salaries, promotions, bonuses, and even the fate of entire schools would depend. It led to teaching to the test, endless drill sessions, and in several cities, outright cheating by teachers who changed their students' answers to exam questions.

In effect, the scripting of teachers' work, along with the system of material incentives designed to make sure that they were following the script, turned what for many teachers was a calling into a job—and a bad job at that. The same has happened in medicine. In our book *Practical Wisdom*, Sharpe and I discuss the case of Dr. David Hilfiker. Here is part of his own description of his work:

The fee schedule had made procedures much more lucrative than in-depth interviews, counseling sessions, or time taken to comfort a hospitalized patient. There were also many important services I performed which had no charge attached whatsoever: returning telephone calls about a child's fever, giving emotional support to a family after a death, going to medical staff meetings, to mention only a few. But despite my conscious disagreement with many of the values assigned by price, I noticed that surgery, procedures, hospital admissions, and emergency-room work slowly became a more and more important part of my practice. Dealing with emotionally hurting patients, taking time to educate patients about the course of their disease and the nature of their treatment, even obtaining a comprehensive medical history, became less central. Not that I consciously changed my routines, but money had powerful ways of bending my perceptions. . . . It is not an exaggeration to say that money seeped into every crack in my life. . . .

Paradoxically, as I did my best to manipulate patients into conforming to the needs of an efficiently run office, it was I who became the object, the machine. . . . I measured myself at the end of the day by what I had produced. . . . I certainly recognized the limited power of money to satisfy me, yet since much of my day was structured around charges and costs and since my income level had become emotionally important to me, money was an important value. Patients' diseases and my service became commodities that were bought and sold at a price.

Here, too, the prospect of a calling—to cure disease and ease suffering—that brought Hilfiker into medicine was disappearing from his everyday experience, which came to look more and more like a job. And it wasn't just Dr. Hilfiker. The growth of for-profit, managed care medical practices in the 1970s encouraged—even compelled—doctors to watch the bottom line. One way to do that was by means of "risk-sharing" agreements forced on doctors by their employers. The managed care organizations would get an annual fee per patient (called "capitation"). If a given patient cost more than that annual fee (because, for example, of repeated referrals to specialists), the managed care organization would suffer a loss. That arrangement incentivized their doctors to keep specialist referrals to a minimum. This risk sharing did not *forbid* doctors from prescribing tests and treatments, but each doctor was given a financial reward for cutting back.

There are legitimate reasons—financial and medical—to worry about doctors who do too much, which the fee-for-service structure of medicine encouraged. But an incentive scheme like "risk-sharing" will turn doctors who do too much into doctors who do too little. What we need, of course, is doctors who do just the right amount. We might say of such doctors that they are good doctors. But is there an incentive structure that will produce the right amount? The incentive for doctors to produce the right amount is their desire to practice medicine well. If they have that desire, no further material incentives are needed. Instead, we just have to make sure that the incentives that are actually in place don't have perverse effects on the quality of medical care. After all, doctors *do* have to make a living. We just want to make sure that what they have to do to make a living doesn't interfere with what it takes to be a good doctor.

I don't want to suggest that offering financial incentives to doctors to withhold services will induce all doctors to do less than they should. But it doesn't have to affect *all* doctors. As Atul Gawande documented in a *New Yorker* article a few years ago, what doctors do is very much influenced by what are the customary practices in their local communities. Some prestigious hospital sets a standard for the proportion of children born by cesarean delivery, or the proportion of joint injuries diagnosed by expensive MRIs instead of less expensive X-rays, and other institutions follow suit. This leads to dramatic regional differences in the frequency with which such procedures are done with little or no difference in the types of cases doctors face— or the outcomes of these cases. So when some doctors start doing too little because they are offered incentives to withhold services, or too much because they are compensated for each procedure, what they do can become the practice norm, so that eventually, even doctors not incentivized to do too little or too much are doing too little or too much.

It may seem obvious that incentivizing doctors to withhold services is a bad idea—one that will lead, inevitably, to inadequate medical care. But it can't be too obvious because, right now, the same mistake is being repeated. In an effort to lower the nation's health bill, health policy experts are advocating the creation of "accountable care organizations," medical groups whose performance is to be measured against high standards of excellence. So far, so good. There is certainly nothing wrong with expecting doctors to be accountable for the quality of their care. But system architects aren't content with establishing high standards and then expecting doctors to try to meet those standards. No. To motivate the pursuit of high standards, they suggest that material incentives be offered to those doctors who meet them. Is there any reason to believe that these efforts will be any different in their results than the efforts to incentivize teachers to produce excellent test results?

It seems that no matter how many times in the past we have gotten evidence that material incentives failed to produce the results we sought from practicing professionals, we turn to them again the next time we want to improve quality. Somehow, system designers repeatedly fail to appreciate that when material incentives are put front and center, other values essential to motivating employees get crowded out. And it is these other values that are responsible for excellent performance. This happens on the factory floor. It happens in teaching. It happens in medicine. And it happens in law.

The 1980s brought a dramatic increase in the commercialization of legal practice by large law firms. Advertising and marketing of firm services grew. New fee-setting practices linked a firm's income to its clients' profits, and lawyer compensation was tied more and more to economic performance. Talk about income and clients' fees, even within the large Wall Street firms, just wasn't done before the 1980s, says Patrick Schiltz, a law professor who used to practice big-firm law. But soon, lawyers talked of little else. Trade publications like *The American Lawyer* began to report regularly on lawyer incomes, publishing extensive surveys that focused on the incomes of associates and partners in big firms. In 1986, the American Bar Association (ABA) was concerned enough to create a Commission on Professionalism, whose report called on the judiciary, the practicing bar, and law schools to take steps to promote public service and "resist the temptation to make the acquisition of wealth a primary goal of law practice."

What happens to law school graduates when they actually go to work for one of these firms is often gradual and subtle. The culture of money making seeps in slowly. No one takes a young lawyer aside and says, "Jane, we here at Smith and Jones are obsessed with money. From this point forward the most important thing in your life has to be billing hours and generating business. Honesty and fairness are okay in moderation, but don't let them interfere with making money."

Schiltz, who, like Dr. Hilfiker, fled his job because of what it was doing to him, went into teaching (at Notre Dame Law School) and tried to prepare his students for what to expect. "You will become unethical," Schiltz warned his students, "a little bit at a time."

Not by "shredding incriminating documents or bribing jurors" but "by cutting a corner here, by stretching the truth a bit there." "It will start," said Schiltz, "with your time sheets and the extraordinary pressure to achieve the mandatory number of billable hours."

> One day, not too long after you start practicing law, you will sit
> down at the end of a long, tiring day and you just won't have much

to show for your efforts in terms of billable hours. . . . You will know that all of the partners will be looking at your monthly time report in a few days, so what you'll do is pad your time sheet just a bit.

The billable hours system provides greater profits for the partners than they can make by themselves. Billable hours are easy-to-monitor indices of hard work. And the system motivates associates to generate extraordinarily large numbers of billable hours, putting moneymaking and promotion at the center of their concerns. Each day, this system makes the merry-go-round of work spin faster, with associates looking over their shoulders, desperate to outwork their peers, hoping to improve their chances at grasping the brass rings of affluence and job security that "making partner" promises.

One effect of the system, says Schiltz, is to undermine the young lawyer's devotion to the interests of the client. To pad your time sheet:

Maybe you will bill a client for ninety minutes for a task that really took you only sixty minutes to perform. However, you will promise yourself that you will repay the client at the first opportunity by doing thirty minutes of work for the client for "free." In this way, you will be "borrowing," not "stealing." . . . And then what will happen is that it will become easier and easier to take these little loans against future work. And then, after a while you will stop paying back these little loans. You will convince yourself that . . . you did such good work that your client should pay a bit more for it.

Another consequence is that the young lawyer's devotion to the truth, and to his colleagues in the firm, will also suffer. The little lies on the time sheets will create the habit of little lies.

> You will get busy and your partner will ask whether you proof-read a lengthy prospectus and you will say yes even though you didn't. And then you will be drafting a brief and you will quote language from a Supreme Court opinion even though you will know that, when read in context, the language does not remotely suggest what you are implying it suggests.

After a couple of years, Schiltz told his students, you'll stop even noticing that lying and cheating have become part of your everyday practice. "Your entire frame of reference will change" and the dozens of quick decisions you make every day will "reflect a set of values that embodies not what is right or wrong but what is profitable, and what you can get away with."

"What is profitable." "What you can get away with." Notice how this plays into the belief that people work (only) for pay. The only way to get people to work hard, work well, and work right is to make it worth their while—to pay them for hard, good work. Just as Adam Smith would have said. And what's the harm? Suppose a lawyer is committed to serving his clients and to serving justice. Making it worth his while will only get him to work harder. Suppose a doctor is committed to easing suffering and curing disease. Making it worth her while will only make her more committed. And making it worth a dedicated teacher's while will only make him more engaged with his task. In other words, if people already have one reason to do something well (their commitment to excellence at their work) and you give them a second reason (financial incentives), this should only make the motivation stronger. It's a simple matter of logic that two reasons are better than one.

If only. For forty years, psychologists and economists have been studying this seemingly logical assumption empirically, and finding that it doesn't hold. Adding financial incentives to situations in which people are motivated to work hard and well without them seems to undermine rather than enhance the motives people already have. Economist Bruno Frey calls it "motivational crowding out." Psychologists Edward Deci, Richard Ryan, and Mark Lepper talk about how "extrinsic" motivation, like the pursuit of money, undermines "intrinsic" motivation.

Here's an example. An Israeli day care center was faced with a problem: more and more parents were coming late—after closing—to pick up their kids. Since the day care center couldn't very well lock up and leave toddlers sitting alone on the steps awaiting their errant parents, they were stuck. Exhortation to come on time did not have the desired effect, so the day care center resorted to a fine for lateness. Now parents would have two reasons to come on time. It was their obligation, and they would pay a fine for failing to meet that obligation.

But the day care center was in for a surprise. When they imposed a fine for lateness, lateness *increased*. Prior to the imposition of a fine, about 25 percent of parents came late. When the fine was introduced, the percentage of latecomers *rose*, to about

33 percent. As the fines continued, the percentage of latecomers continued to go up, reaching about 40 percent by the sixteenth week.

Why did the fines have this paradoxical effect? To many of the parents, it seemed that a fine was just a price (indeed, "A Fine Is a Price" was the title of the article reporting this finding). We know that a fine is not a price. A price is what you pay for a service or a good. It's an exchange between willing participants. A fine, in contrast, is punishment for a transgression. A $25 parking ticket is not the price for parking; it's the penalty for parking where parking is not permitted. But there is nothing to stop people from interpreting a fine as a price. If it costs you $30 to park in a downtown garage, you might well calculate that it's cheaper to park illegally on the street. Any notion of moral sanction is lost. You're not doing the "wrong" thing; you're doing the economical thing. And to get you to stop, we'll have to make the fine (price) for parking illegally higher than the price for parking in a garage.

That's exactly what happened in the day care centers. Prior to the imposition of fines, parents knew it was wrong to come late. Obviously, many of the parents did not regard this transgression as serious enough to get them to stop committing it, but there was no question that what they were doing was wrong. But when fines were introduced, the moral dimension of their behavior disappeared. It was now a straightforward financial calculation. "They're giving me permission to be late. Is it worth $25? Is that a good price to pay to let me stay in the office a few minutes longer? Sure is!" The fine allows parents to reframe their behavior as an exchange of a fee (the "fine") for a "service" (fifteen minutes of extra care). The fines *de*moralized what had previously been a moral act. And this is what incentives can do in general. They can change the question in people's minds from "Is this right or wrong?" to "Is this worth the price?"

Once lost, this moral dimension is hard to recover. When, near the end of the study, the fines for lateness were discontinued, lateness became even more prevalent. By the end of the study, the incidence of lateness had almost doubled. It's as though the introduction of fines permanently altered parents' framing of the situation from a moral transaction to an economic one. When the fines were lifted, lateness simply became a better deal.

There is certainly nothing foolish about imposing a fine for lateness. Any one of us might have reached for exactly this tool. But it is only a small step down a slippery slope from the Israeli day care center to teachers who teach to the test and doctors who treat with their eyes firmly fixed on the bottom line.

Another example of the demoralizing effects of incentives comes from a study of the willingness of Swiss citizens to have nuclear waste dumps in their communities. In the early 1990s, Switzerland was getting ready to have a national referendum about where it would site nuclear waste dumps. Citizens had strong views on the issue and were well informed. The researchers went door-to-door, asking people whether they would be willing to have a waste dump in their community. An astonishing 50 percent of respondents said yes—this despite the fact that people generally thought such a dump was potentially dangerous and would lower the value of their property. The dumps had to go somewhere, and like it or not, people had obligations as citizens.

The researchers then asked a slightly different question: People were asked whether, if they were given an annual payment equivalent to six weeks worth of an average Swiss salary, they would be willing to have the dumps in their communities. This incentive gave people who already had one reason to say yes—their obligations as citizens—a second reason. Yet, in response to this question, only 25 percent of respondents agreed. Adding the financial incentive cut acceptance in half.

These studies of Israeli parents and Swiss citizens are surprising. You're more likely to order a dish that tastes good and is good for you than one that just tastes good. You're more likely to buy a car that's reliable and fuel efficient than one that's just reliable. But when the parents at the day care center were given a second reason to be on time—the fines—it undermined their first reason, that it was the right thing to do. And the Swiss who were given two reasons to accept a nuclear waste site were *less* likely to say yes than those only given one. So reasons don't always add; sometimes, they compete.

A study by James Heyman and Dan Ariely makes a similar point. People were asked if they would be willing to help load a couch onto a van. Some were offered a modest fee and some were not. Participants in the study can construe the task they face either as a social transaction (doing someone a favor) or a financial one (working for a fee). Absent the offer of a fee, they were inclined to view the situation in social terms, and agree to help. The offer of a fee induced the participants to reframe the transaction as financial. Now the fee had better be substantial.

It might seem that if you are inclined to do someone a favor, the offer of compensation should only give you a second reason to do what you were inclined to do already. Again, two reasons are better than one. Except that they're not. The offer of money tells people implicitly that they are operating in the financial/ commercial domain, not the social domain. The offer of money leads them to ask, "Is this worth my time and effort?" That is not a question they ask themselves when someone asks them for a favor. Thus, social motives and financial ones compete.

This sort of motivational competition doesn't always happen, and despite years of empirical evidence, I don't think we fully understand it yet. But clearly, the lesson is that incentives can be a dangerous weapon. A critic of this research might say that the problem is not incentives, but dumb incentives. No doubt, some incentives are dumber than others. But no incentives can ever be smart enough to substitute for people who do the right thing *because* it's the right thing. Why are incentives such a blunt instrument?

The main reason is that most jobs—and certainly all jobs involving substantial interactions with other people—are organized around what are called *incomplete* contracts. Some of the job duties are specified explicitly, but many are not. Doctors prevent disease, diagnose it, treat it, and ease suffering. But exactly how they do these things is left to them to figure out— with guidelines, of course, but only guidelines. And how they interact with their patients is left for them to figure out. Lawyers serve their clients, but how they do that—when and how they counsel, when and how they advocate—is up to them. Teachers impart knowledge, but the best way to reach each child is left for them to judge. Being caring and sensitive to patients and their families is not part of our hospital janitors' "contract," nor are there any rules or procedures that specify how to be caring.

Detailed scripts and rules may enable us to make contracts that are more complete, but moving in that direction will compromise the quality of the services that doctors, lawyers, teachers, and even custodians provide. More complete contracts allow us to incentivize what we think we want ("perform tasks A, B, and C in the manner X, Y, and Z and you get a bonus"). But what we really want is to "make a good faith effort to do whatever it takes to achieve our objective." We can have confidence that our service providers will do "whatever it takes" only if they have the will to do the right thing. How much we depend on this good faith on the part of employees, even in factory, assembly-line settings, is revealed by a kind of union protest that used to be popular many years ago. When a dispute with management arose, instead of going out on strike, unions would sometimes resort to "working to rule." Employees did exactly what was specified in their contracts—and nothing more. Perhaps predictably, such work-to-rule actions paralyzed production.

When we lose confidence that people have the will to do the right thing, and we turn to incentives, we find that we get what we pay for. Teachers teach to the test, so that test scores go up without students learning more. Doctors do more, or fewer, procedures (depending on the incentives) without improving the quality of medical care. Custodians just "do their jobs," leaving unhappy, uncomfortable patients in their wake. As economist Fred Hirsch said forty years ago, "the more that is written in contracts, the less can be expected without them; the more you write it down, the less is taken, or expected, on trust." The solution to incomplete contracts is not more complete ones; it is a nurturing of workplace relationships in which people want to do right by the clients, patients, students, and customers they serve.

The philosopher turned social scientist William Sullivan captured much of this concept in his book *Work and Integrity*. His argument in the book is largely that as a society we have come to think that we can do without the integrity of professionals if we can just create a good set of practice rules, coupled with a smart scheme of incentives. We can't. There is really no substitute for the integrity that inspires people to do good work because they want to do good work. And the more we rely on incentives as substitutes for integrity, the more we will need to rely on them as substitutes for integrity. We may tell ourselves that all we're doing with our incentives is taking advantage of what we know about human nature. That's what Adam Smith would have said. But in fact, what we're doing is changing human nature.

And we're not merely changing it; we're impoverishing it.

4 The Technology of Ideas

"Human Nature" as a Battle Between Metaphors

On the campus where I teach, every time a new building is built or an old one is substantially renovated, an issue arises about where to locate the asphalt walkways that go between that building and other campus locations. One school of thought suggests that the placement of walkways should be part of the building plan. But a second school, no doubt having observed many asphalt paths that lie unused near trails of dirt where once there had been grass, has the view that you build the building, watch where people walk, and put the asphalt where the grass has been worn thin. Proponents of the first view are folks we might call "theory driven." Guided by some sense of efficient movement, aesthetics, or both, they are inclined to do the "ideal" thing, and have people conform to it. Proponents of the second view are folks we might call "data driven." They let the users of the space tell them, with their behavior, what the "ideal" thing is.

When done right, all of science is an ongoing conversation between theory and data. The point of theories in science is to organize and explain the facts. Facts without organizing theories are close to useless. But theories must ultimately be accountable to, and conform to, the facts. And new facts force us to modify or discard inadequate theories.

That's the ideal. But in real life, things don't always work out this way. At least in the social sciences, proposing theories, rather than being beholden to facts, can shape facts in a way that strengthens the theories. You build that path and then force people to walk on it, perhaps by roping off the grass.

"If you build it, they will come." This is the mantra that the main character in the movie *Field of Dreams* keeps hearing as he turns his farmland into a baseball park in the middle of nowhere. He builds it, and they *do* come. In this chapter, I will try to show that at least sometimes, when social scientists build theories, the people come. That is, the people are nudged into behaving in ways that support the theories. This chapter, then, is an attempt to resolve a battle between these metaphors. The "watch where they walk, then pave it" metaphor argues that the empirical data shape the theories people develop. The "if you build it, they will come" metaphor argues that theories shape data. I will attempt to defend the second metaphor.

The battle here is one that has been going on in more familiar territory for years. Does the market cater to consumer desires or does it create consumer desires? Do the media cater to people's tastes in news and entertainment or do the media create those tastes? We are all accustomed to the difficulties surrounding discussion of these issues in modern society, and we may all have fairly strong opinions about the "cater/create" debate. Questions of just this sort are all around us, and finding the right answer to them can have profound consequences for the future of society.

In a sense, the distinction I'm making is between discovery and invention. Discoveries tell us things about how the world works. Inventions use those discoveries to create objects or processes that make the world work differently. The discovery of pathogens leads to the invention of antibiotics. The discovery of nuclear energy leads to bombs, power plants, and medical procedures. The discovery of the genome leads, or will lead, to untold changes in almost every part of our lives. Of course, discoveries also change the world, by changing how we understand it and live in it, but they rarely change the world by themselves.

In the natural sciences, the distinction between discovery and invention is pretty clear, though there are occasional tough cases. For example, when Myriad Genetics Corporation, in Utah, discovered BRCA1 and BRCA2 DNA, which predisposes women to breast and ovarian cancer, they patented their discovery, at least when extracted from the body. These patents meant that researchers could not use the isolated DNA without permission from the company. It also meant that the company controlled the development and use of diagnostic tests that depended on this DNA. This patenting was met with court challenges that it survived until it was struck down by the Supreme Court in June 2013. The courts had long held that natural products, natural phenomena, and laws of nature could not be patented, unless some kind of "inventive" step gave them "markedly different characteristics from any found in nature." Thus, discoveries cannot be patented, but inventions can. The dispute in the BRCA DNA case was basically whether the isolation of this material constituted a discovery or an invention—whether it was a contribution to basic science or a piece of technology.

The distinction between discovery and invention is crucial, and not just because it affects who gets to earn how much money from what. When a scientist, or anyone else, discovers something, it doesn't occur to us to ask whether that discovery *should* exist. In other words, though discoveries often have moral implications, they do not, by themselves, have moral dimensions. If someone were to suggest that the Higgs boson shouldn't exist, we'd wonder what mind-altering substance he'd ingested. Inventions, in contrast, are a whole other story. Inventions characteristically have moral dimensions. We routinely ask whether they should exist. We wonder what's good (life improving) about them, and what the drawbacks are. We debate whether their wide distribution should go forward, and if so, with what kind of regulation.

So is a theory about human nature a discovery, or is it an invention? I believe that often, it is more invention than discovery. I think that ideas, like Adam Smith's, about what motivates people to work have shaped the nature of the workplace. I think they have shaped the workplace in directions that are unfortunate. What this means is that instead of walking around thinking that "well, work just is what it is, and we have to deal with it," we should be asking whether the way work is is the way it should be. My answer to that question is an unequivocal no.

We've seen how potentially good work situations, in education, medicine, or law, can easily turn into bad ones, either from excessive oversight and regulation or from excessive reliance on material incentives. Why do things like this happen? Given what people want from their work, and what makes customers, clients, patients, and students satisfied, why is so much work so impoverished? The answer, I think, is illustrated by the Keynes quote with which the book began:

> The ideas of economists and political philosophers, both when they are right and when they are wrong, are more powerful than is commonly understood. Indeed the world is ruled by little else. Practical men, who believe themselves to be quite exempt from any intellectual influences, are usually the slaves of some defunct economist.

The ideas that Keynes is talking about are ideas about human nature—about what people care about, and what they aspire to. And like fish that don't know they live in water, we live with such ideas about human nature that are so pervasive that we don't even realize there's another way to look at ourselves.

Where do our ideas about human nature come from? Where once they may have come from our parents, our community leaders, and our religious texts, these days, they come mostly from science—specifically from social science. Social science has created a "technology" of ideas about human nature. To grasp fully how the majority of our work became so impoverished, it is essential to understand this "idea technology"—what it is, how it works, and how it changes us.

Idea Technology

We live in a culture and an age in which the influence of scientific technology is obvious and overwhelming. Whether it's

laptops, smart phones, and tablets, or MRI scans, gene modifications, and designer drugs, adjusting to technology is a brute
and insistent fact of daily life. Some of us embrace technology
enthusiastically, and some of us do it grudgingly, but everyone
does it.

The technology of smart phones and MRIs—the technology
of things—is what most of us think of when we think about the
modern impact of science. But in addition to creating things,
science creates concepts, ways of understanding the world and
our place in it, that have an enormous effect on how we think
and act. If we understand birth defects as acts of God, we pray.
If we understand them as acts of chance, we grit our teeth and
roll the dice. If we understand them as the product of prenatal
neglect, we take better care of pregnant women.

It hardly needs to be said that people are profoundly affected
by the material conditions of their lives—by the affluence of the
societies they inhabit. The availability of necessities like food
and shelter and the means by which individuals may obtain
them makes all other influences on life seem insignificant.
People without food will starve whether they accept their conditions beatifically as God's will, accept them with depressed
resignation as indications of their own inadequacy, or respond
to them in anger at social injustice. No matter what ideas people
appeal to when they explain their lack of food, their bellies
remain empty.

And yet it is clear that ideas also matter, and they matter a
lot, even in the case of an obvious material condition like the
availability of food. What a squirrel foraging for food in the park

does in times of scarcity has nothing to do with how the squirrel understands this scarcity. The squirrel is not about to pray for food, cultivate trees, or organize other squirrels to rise up in protest against people who have polluted the environment and diminished its food sources; the squirrel just forages for food. But what people do about their lack of food depends a great deal on how they understand it. Ideas have much to do with whether massive food shortages yield resignation or revolution.

If we understand the concept of "technology" broadly, as the use of human intelligence to create objects or processes that change the conditions of daily life, then it seems clear that ideas are no less products of technology than are computers. However, there are two things about idea technology that make it different from most "thing technology." First, because ideas are not objects, to be seen, purchased, and touched, they can suffuse through the culture and have profound effects on people before they are even noticed. Second, ideas, unlike things, can have profound effects on people *even if the ideas are false*. Smart phones, designer drugs, and the like generally don't affect people's lives unless they do what they were designed to do. Companies can't sell technological objects that fail—at least not for very long. Technological objects may do bad things that people don't want them to do, but at least there is little reason to worry about them unless they can also do the things they were designed to do in the first place. In contrast, false ideas can affect how people act, just as long as people believe them. Following philosopher Karl Marx, let's call instances of idea technology based on untrue ideas "ideology." Because idea technology often goes unnoticed, and because it can have profound effects even when it's false—when it is ideology—it is in some respects more profound in its influence than the thing technology whose effects people are so accustomed to worrying about.

Now, wait a minute, you might say. Why aren't ideas just like things? The hallmark of science is that it operates in the world of testable hypotheses. That is, if you have an idea, you test it, and if it fails the test, it also disappears, just like bad thing technology. So there's no need to worry about a technology of false ideas. False ideas will just die of "natural causes." Right?

Alas, no. Ideology bears a large measure of the responsibility for the nature of our work. Look at another quote from Adam Smith:

> The man whose life is spent in a few simple operations . . . has no occasion to exert his understanding, or to exercise his invention in finding out expedients for difficulties which never occur. He naturally loses, therefore, the habit of such exertion and generally becomes as stupid and ignorant as it is possible for a human creature to be.

Smith says of the man who works on the assembly lines that "He naturally loses, therefore, the habit of such exertion and generally becomes as stupid and ignorant as it is possible for a human creature to be." The key things to notice about this statement are the words "loses" and "becomes." Here is Smith, the father of the assumption that people are basically lazy and work only for pay, saying that work in a factory will cause people to "lose" something, and "become" something. So what is it that they *had* before entering the factory that they "lost"? And what is it that they *were* before entering the factory that was different from what they "became"? Right here in this quote we see evidence that Smith believed that what people were like as workers depended on the conditions of their work. And yet, over the years, this nuanced understanding of human nature as the product of the human environment got lost. As a result of this lost subtlety, creating the soulless, dehumanizing workplaces that most people faced needed no justification except for economic efficiency. It wasn't changing people. It wasn't depriving people of anything. It was simply taking people as they were and using their labor with maximum efficiency.

We now know that it *was* changing people. A classic article by Melvin Kohn and Carmi Schooler, published thirty years ago, showed as much: They showed that work over which people exercise some discretion and control leads to cognitive flexibility and to an engaged orientation to self and society; in contrast, excessively monitored, oppressively supervised working conditions lead to distress. More recently, in a similar vein, Sanford DeVoe and Jeffrey Pfeffer have shown that the way in which people are compensated changes them. Professionals who bill by the hour, like lawyers and consultants, start putting a price on their time, even when they aren't at work. An evening spent with friends watching a ball game has "costs" in legal fees and consulting fees forgone. So a person who bills by the hour becomes a different person than she was before she started working in that way.

Also striking is a series of studies by Chip Heath that show that even when people don't think of *themselves* as primarily motivated by material incentives, they think that pretty much *everyone* else is. Heath surveyed students taking the Law School Admissions Test (LSAT). They were asked to describe their own motives for pursuing a legal career, and then to speculate about the motives of their peers. Sixty-four percent said that they were pursuing a legal career because it was intellectually appealing or because they had always been interested in the law, but only 12 percent thought that was true of their peers. Instead, 62 percent speculated that their peers were pursuing a legal career because of financial rewards. So we may tell ourselves that we are exceptional in caring about things besides money, which in turn makes it easier for us to organize the work of others entirely based on monetary incentives.

Along similar lines, Heath reports results from the General Social Survey (GSS). For more than twenty-five years, the GSS has asked a sample of adults to rank the importance of five different aspects of their jobs: pay, security, free time, chances for advancement, and "important work" that "gives a feeling of accomplishment." Year after year, "important work" is, on average, ranked first by more than 50 percent of the individual respondents. Pay typically ranks third. Yet, in the late 1980s, when the GSS asked respondents about the role of material incentives for others, people generally believed that pay was quite important.

So ideas change people. Our pressing question is: How can idea technology take root, even when the ideas are false—even when they are ideology? How can we make ourselves aware of ideology in action? And finally, how can we change it?

The term "ideology" has not been used consistently over time. The term's history began in France in the eighteenth century, coined to denote a "science of ideas." People whom the French emperor Napoleon termed *ideologues* were so in love with ideas that they ignored empirical evidence, sometimes right in front of their noses, that might contradict those ideas. A more recent manifestation of this view of people as so committed to ideas that they ignore evidence can be found in Jonathan Haidt's *The Righteous Mind*, which argues that people's moral commitments stem not from reason and reflection, but from deep-seated intuitions of which they are largely unaware. That is, people *believe* they make moral judgments by thinking the issues through, using reason to sift through evidence and arguments as a judge of pros and cons. But, in fact, Haidt tells us, they have a moral position before they ever turn their thinking loose on an issue. They use reason as a lawyer does—to make a case for what they already believe, and not as a judge, to tell them what they ought to believe. This orientation can lead not only to ignoring evidence, but to distorting it, a result of what psychologist Lee Ross called "naive realism." The naive realist is someone who thinks that "I see things as they are; people who disagree with me are distorting the truth."

Somewhat akin to what Ross dubbed naive realism, a century earlier, Marx appropriated the term "ideology" to identify what he called "false consciousness." So for Marx, ideologues weren't just ignoring evidence to preserve their pet theories; they were *distorting* evidence to conform to what they already believed, or were conditioned by their circumstances to believe, or wanted to believe. And in Marx's case, he was very much interested in the nature of work, since his focus was on how the owners of businesses were exploiting the people who actually did the work.

So how does ideology happen? You would think that in the scientific, big-data age in which we live, eventually the empirical evidence would win the day, and good data would drive out bad ideas. The history of science is a history of one mistaken theory after another, with careful collection and interpretation of data the engine for correcting these mistakes. Better data and theories drive out worse ones, and progress is made. Why does this not happen in the case of theories about human nature?

Well, sometimes it does. Psychologists have made much progress over the years in understanding perception, memory, thinking, language use and comprehension, cognitive and social development, learning, and various types of emotional and cognitive disorders in exactly the same way that natural sciences make progress in their domains. Good data drive out bad theories. But there's a crucial difference between theories about planets, atoms, genes, and diseases and theories about at least some aspects of human nature. Planets don't care what scientists say about their behavior. They move around the sun with complete indifference to how physicists and astronomers theorize about them. Genes are indifferent to our theories about them also. But this is not true of people. Theories about human nature can actually produce changes in how people behave. What this means is that a theory that is false can *become* true simply by people believing it's true. The result is that, instead of good data driving out bad data and theories, bad data change social practices until the data become good data, and the theories are validated.

How does ideology become true in this way? There are three basic dynamics. The first way ideology becomes true is by changing how people think about their own actions. For example, someone who volunteered every week in a homeless shelter might one day read a book that tells him it is human nature to be selfish. He might then say to himself, "I thought I was acting altruistically. Now social scientists are telling me that I work in a homeless shelter for ego gratification." Or someone on her way to work might say, "I thought I showed up for work every day eager to be challenged and do a good job that improves someone's life. Now social scientists are telling me it's all about the money." If this kind of reconstrual takes place, nothing outside the person necessarily changes. The person simply understands her actions differently. But of course, how we understand our past actions is likely to affect our future actions. It isn't hard to imagine, for example, that hospital custodians like Luke, Ben, Carlotta, and Corey—already a rare breed—will disappear entirely as the ideology that people work only for pay penetrates our culture even more than it already has.

The second mechanism by which ideology becomes true is via what is called the "self-fulfilling prophecy." Here, ideology changes how other people respond to the actor, which, in turn, changes what the actor does in the future. A classic demonstration of this self-fulfilling mechanism in action was reported by

Mark Snyder and Elizabeth Tanke in 1977. In this study, groups of men were shown a photo of either an attractive or an unattractive woman. They then had a ten-minute phone conversation with a woman they were led to believe was the woman in the photo (she was not). After the conversation, those who thought they were talking to the attractive woman rated her as more likeable than those who thought they were talking to the unattractive woman. No surprise here. The surprise came next. Tapes of the conversations were played for other participants who had not seen photographs of the woman or been told anything about her attractiveness. They, too, judged the "attractive" woman as more likeable, friendly, and sociable than the unattractive one.

Think about this result. Somehow, thinking their interview subject was attractive led interviewers to conduct their interviews in a way that led third parties who listened to the interview to come to the same conclusion. In effect, the interviewers collected "data" in a way that was biased by their initial beliefs.

The phrase "self-fulfilling prophecy" was coined by sociologist Robert Merton in 1948. He discussed examples of how theories that initially do not describe the world accurately can become descriptive if they are acted upon. In essence, a "self-fulfilling prophecy" is "a *false* definition of the situation evoking a new behavior that makes the originally false conception come *true*."

Merton went on to explore the causal link between a prophecy and its subsequent confirmation. For instance, Merton cited the then prevalent notion that black workers were "unsuitable" to be members of labor unions. With their "low standard of living" and willingness to "take jobs at less than prevailing wages," these laborers became "traitors to the working class." What the exclusionary unions failed to recognize, argued Merton, is that the very act of excluding black workers from the union caused the behavior that seems to confirm the hypothesis. Not being members of the union during a strike, black workers would cross the picket line to fill the labor void, breaking the strike, ostensibly vindicating the original claim as to their unsuitability for union membership. What was originally a false hypothesis—an ideology—changed the situation, configuring it in ways that appeared to validate it.

The parallel of this kind of process in the workplace is clear. You start out believing that people are basically lazy, don't want to work, and care only about their pay when they do. Based on this belief, you create a workplace that is focused only on efficiency, with jobs that are mindlessly repetitive, counting on the paycheck to motivate the workers. Lo and behold, in an environment like that, all that matters to workers is their pay.

Another notable example of this process is the teacher who pays more attention and works harder with children identified as "smart" than children identified as "slow," thereby making the "smart" ones smarter. Thus, being labeled as "smart" or "slow" does not in itself make kids smarter or slower. The teacher's behavior must also change accordingly. Perhaps the best-known demonstration of the self-fulfilling prophecy in education is shown in the research conducted by Robert Rosenthal and Lenore Jacobson on the effects of teacher expectations on student performance. Unbeknownst to the teachers in the study, the researchers randomly assigned certain students in an elementary school classroom to the "spurter" condition. These students supposedly had taken a diagnostic test at the end of the preceding school year that identified them as having the potential for impressive academic gains. No such test had actually been administered. Nonetheless, the students who'd been labeled as spurters *did* manifest more impressive gains than average by the end of the school year. High expectations from the teacher somehow resulted in high student achievement, which the authors termed the "Pygmalion Effect." In short, Rosenthal and Jacobson argued, the labeling of certain students as promising became a self-fulfilling prophecy by changing the way teachers taught. This finding has been highly influential in both the fields of psychology and education.

Years later, Lee Jussim and colleagues followed up on this line of inquiry by assessing specific ways in which teacher expectations affect student performance and the specific contexts in which such expectations have the most marked effects. Though they found evidence supporting the self-fulfilling prophecy framework laid out by Rosenthal and Jacobson, they also identified bounds to the pervasiveness and power of the self-fulfilling prophecy. Jussim found that such prophecies are not all-pervading, and the magnitude of the effects, though significant, is often modest.

It is perhaps not surprising that the "Pygmalion effects" are not large. After all, the kids may get one subtle message about their ability in school but quite a different one at home from their doting parents. But if the message were delivered more consistently, across all the domains of a child's experience, then the effects might be very large indeed.

Can such a pervasive message be sent? Well, think about the way in which many psychologists and educators talk about intelligence. As you probably know, there is some evidence, and much belief, that individual differences in intelligence are innate, and unmodifiable. Some people win the genetic lottery and some lose it. It isn't hard to imagine that if this idea about intelligence became commonplace, parents would take their cue from teachers and give their kids the same messages the kids were getting in school. But is this understanding of intelligence true, or is it ideology?

I suppose the jury is still out to some degree, but consider the work of psychologist Carol Dweck, summarized in her book *Mindset*. Dweck has discovered that we can distinguish among children based on the goals that seem to be operating while they learn. Some kids have what Dweck calls performance goals. These kids want to do well on tests. They want social approval. Other kids have what she calls mastery goals. These kids want to encounter things that they can't do and to learn from their failures. As Dweck puts it, performance-oriented children want to *prove* their ability while mastery-oriented children want to *improve* their ability.

Children with performance goals avoid challenges. Children with mastery goals seek challenges. Children with performance goals respond to failure by giving up. Children with mastery goals respond to failure by working harder. What this means is that children with mastery goals learn more, and get smarter, than children with performance goals.

Dweck has shown that what lies beneath these two orientations is a pair of quite different conceptions or "theories" children have of the nature of intelligence. Some children believe that intelligence is essentially immutable—that it is a fixed entity. These are the children who tend to be performance oriented. What's the point of seeking challenges and risking failure if you can't get any smarter? Other children believe that intelligence is not fixed—that it is incremental and people *can* get smarter. These children tend to be mastery oriented, seeking in their schoolwork to do what they believe is possible for everyone. So is intelligence fixed? Partly, that depends on whether you believe it's fixed. What this means is that the theory that intelligence is fixed may well be ideology.

Not surprisingly, results parallel to Dweck's have been found throughout the workplace. Peter Heslin, Gary Latham, and Don VandeWalle did a series of studies of how managers manage their employees. They discovered that managers also seemed to have either fixed or incremental theories of employee ability. If managers had a fixed theory of ability, they were less likely to notice changes in employee performance, and less likely to provide feedback and coaching aimed at improvement, than if they had an incremental theory of ability. What's the point, they seemed to think, of trying to improve something that can't be changed. It's like trying to improve someone's height by encouraging him to grow. But you can see the feedback loop that such an attitude creates. The manager doesn't think performance can be improved, so she does nothing to try to improve performance. Lo and behold, performance does not improve, and her theory is thereby confirmed.

To a large degree, the effects of ideology on how people act will depend on how broadly, how pervasively and how saliently it is purveyed in a culture. When it lives in isolated places, its effects will likely be small and correctable. But when it's in the water supply—when it is everywhere—its effects will likely be much more profound. In support of this point, psychologist Richard Nisbett has shown that entire cultures can be differentiated from one another by the extent to which they are guided by the belief that either intelligence is fixed or that it grows. And studies of intellectual development across these different cultures show that kids living in a culture with a "growth mindset" exhibit more intellectual development than kids living in a culture with a "fixed mindset."

This brings us to the final mechanism by which ideology can have an influence. This mechanism—the one that I believe has the most profound effects on our working environments and beyond—operates to change institutional structures in a way that is consistent with the ideology. The industrialist believes that workers are only motivated to work by wages and then constructs an assembly line that reduces work to such meaningless bits that there is no reason to work aside from the wages. The politician believes that self-interest motivates all behavior, that people are entitled to keep the spoils of their labors, and that people deserve what they get and get what they deserve. Said politician helps enact policies that erode or destroy the social safety net. As a result, people start acting exclusively as self-interested individuals. "If it's up to me to put a roof over our heads, put food on the table, and make sure there's money to pay the doctor and the kids' college tuition bills, then I'd better make sure I take care of myself." When social structures are shaped by ideology, ideology can change the world, sometimes in devastating, far-reaching ways.

We must be especially vigilant about ideology embedded in social structures. It is much harder to change social structures than it is to change how people think about themselves, which psychotherapy may effectively address, or how they think about others, which education may effectively address. Moreover, because social structures affect multitudes rather than individuals, when these structures embody ideology, the effects of that ideology can be pervasive.

It is not hard to imagine how, guided by the ideology fostered by Adam Smith and then elaborated and extended by others, people would come to understand virtually all their behavior, including their relations with their work, and their relations and responsibilities to others, in terms of operative incentives. And as a result, the nature of people's relation to their work and to others would change. In a world like this, we would not have to worry that financial motives would crowd out moral ones as people thought about when to pick up their kids from daycare, or whether to allow nuclear waste dumps in their communities, because the moral ones would already have disappeared.

Consider the character of recent debates about whether to extend unemployment benefits to Americans who are still unable to find work as the economy limps toward recovery. The lives of the unemployed are a struggle even with these benefits; they are close to unmanageable without them. Yet many in the federal government resist. The main argument against extending benefits? Giving people unemployment benefits will undermine their incentive to work. Why work if you can get paid for not working? Built into this argument, of course, is Adam Smith's view that the only reason that people work is for the wage, and if they don't need the wage, they won't work. No one states this view explicitly, because it is so pervasive that it doesn't need to be stated. This is ideology at its most pernicious.

Psychologist Dale Miller has presented evidence of the pervasiveness of what he calls the "norm of self-interest" in American society. College students assume, incorrectly, that women will have stronger views about abortion issues than men and that students under the age of twenty-one will have stronger views about the legal drinking age than those over twenty-one, because women and minors have a stake in those issues that men and older students do not. The possibility that one's views could be shaped by conceptions of justice or fairness, rather than self-interest, does not occur to most people. And yet they are. Empathy, and care and concern for the well-being of others, are routine parts of most people's character. Yet they are in danger of being crowded out by exclusive concern for self-interest—a concern that is encouraged by the incentive-based structure of the workplace.

Even Adam Smith understood that there was more to human nature than self-interest. *The Wealth of Nations* followed another book, *The Theory of Moral Sentiments*, in which he suggested that a certain natural sympathy for one's fellow human beings provided needed restraints on what people would do if they were left free to "barter, truck, and exchange one thing for another." Smith's view, largely forgotten by modernity, was that efficient market transactions were parasitic on aspects of character developed through nonmarket social relations. Smith was right about the importance of "moral sentiments" but wrong about how "natural" they are. In a market-dominated society, in which every aspect of what people do is "incentivized," these "moral sentiments" may disappear so that nothing can rein in self-interest.

Economist and philosopher Amartya Sen has argued that the concern for doing the right thing originates from a source that the logic of self-interest and incentives cannot encompass. He calls that source of concern "commitment." To act out of commitment is to do what one thinks is right, regardless of whether it promotes one's own material circumstances. Acts of commitment include doing one's job to the best of one's ability—going beyond the terms of the contract—even if no one is watching and there is nothing to gain from it. They include refusing to price gouge during times of shortage, refusing to capitalize on fortuitous circumstances at the expense of others, willingness to tolerate nuclear waste dumps in one's community, and coming to pick up one's toddlers from daycare on time.

The concept of ideology, and the self-fulfilling feedback loops that ideology can give rise to, helps explain, I think, why it is that most workplaces have come to be dominated by excessive reliance on close supervision, routinized work, and incentives. If you think that people lack the skill for wise judgment on the job, you impose detailed rules of conduct. As a consequence, people never get the opportunity to develop wise judgment. Your lack of faith in the skills of the people you oversee is validated, leading you to impose still more rules and still greater oversight. And if you think that people lack the will to do their work in pursuit of the right aims, you create incentives that enable people to do well by doing good. In so doing, you undermine whatever motivation people might have to do the right thing *because* it is the right thing. Once again, your lack of confidence is validated. Instead of putting in place procedures that nurture people's desire to do meaningful work, the manager, convinced that such attributes are a very slender reed on which to build and run an organization, puts practices in place that undermine them. Before long, meaningful work disappears—from the classroom, from the courtroom, and from the examination room.

Acts of commitment, like the ones Sen describes, occur routinely. They hold society together. But because of the self-fulfilling character of ideology, we should not be sanguine that they will persist. We should not be confident that the distortion that dominates current thinking about work and workers will reveal itself and be corrected as the sciences of human nature progress. Unless there is a collective effort to combat this ideology, we will all become the lazy, selfish pursuers of self-interest, not just in work but in our lives as a whole, that at least some social scientists have assumed we always were. So the question becomes: What can we do?

In his book *A Conflict of Visions*, Thomas Sowell distinguishes between what he calls "constrained" and "unconstrained" visions of human nature. The constrained vision, put forth by philosopher Thomas Hobbes, focuses on the selfish, aggressive dark side of human nature, and assumes that we cannot change human nature but must instead impose constraints through an all-powerful state, the Leviathan. The unconstrained vision, perhaps best exemplified by Jean-Jacques Rousseau, sees enormous human possibility and condemns the state for subverting all that is good in human nature.

I think that both Hobbes and Rousseau are wrong. "Nature" dramatically underspecifies the character of human beings. Within broad limits, we are what society expects us to be. If society asks little from us, it gets little. It is clear that, under these circumstances, we must be sure that we have arranged rules and incentives in a way that induces people to act in ways that serve the objectives of the rule makers and the incentive setters. If society asks more of us, and arranges its social institutions appropriately, it will get more. As anthropologist Clifford Geertz observed, human beings are "unfinished animals." What we can reasonably expect of people depends on how our social institutions "finish" them.

The idea technology that dominates our age is a fiction; it is ideology. But it is a powerful fiction, and it becomes less and less fictional as it increasingly pervades our institutions and crowds out other types of relations between us and our work. Because of its self-fulfilling character, we cannot expect this fiction to die of natural causes. To kill it, we must nourish the alternatives. And that will not be easy.

5 The Future of Work: Designing Human Nature

A scorpion wants to cross the river, but it can't swim. It goes up to a frog, who can swim, and asks for a ride. The frog says, "If I give you a ride on my back you'll go and sting me."

The scorpion replies, "It would not be in my interest to sting you, since, as I'll be on your back, we both would drown."

The frog thinks about this logic for a while and accepts the deal. It takes the scorpion on its back and braves the waters, but halfway over it feels a burning pain in its side and realizes the scorpion has stung it after all. As they both sink beneath the waves, the frog cries out, "Why'd you sting me, Mr. Scorpion? For now we will both drown."

The scorpion replies, "I can't help it. It's in my nature."

Neil Jordan, *The Crying Game* (1992)
after an original folktale of uncertain origin

Human beings are not scorpions. People aren't stuck being one way or another. But nor are they free to invent themselves without constraint. When we give shape to our social institutions—our schools, our communities and yes, our workplaces—we also shape human nature. Thus, human nature is to a significant degree the product of human design. If we design workplaces that permit people to do work they value, we will be designing a human nature that values work. If we design workplaces that permit people to find meaning in their work, we will be designing a human nature that values work.

Why should we design such workplaces? We've already seen that good workplaces enable people to do good work. Their customers and clients benefit and so do their employers. And there is a second good reason. When people are able to do work they value, it makes them happy. It enhances their well-being. Much more than the material benefits that come from the incentive schemes that employers substitute for good work. Why wouldn't we want to design a workplace that enables its inhabitants to get real satisfaction out of the time they spend there?

We have missed this opportunity thus far partly because of the ideology that tells us that people don't want to work. But we've also missed the opportunity because we've embraced a notion of production efficiency that is much too narrow. Economists think of efficiency in terms of dollars. It's the value of output per unit of input. But suppose we defined efficiency in terms of well-being instead. Presumably, the people who purchase goods and services experience gains in their well-being, because otherwise they wouldn't have made the purchase. So this more expansively defined output includes the dollar value of goods and services plus the satisfaction those goods and services bring. But what about the costs of the inputs? Well, in addition to the dollar costs of labor and materials, we must add the psychic costs experienced by workers doing jobs they hate. If we redesigned workplaces so that workers liked their work, these psychic costs would become psychic benefits. Why on earth wouldn't we do this?

It places a great burden on us when we appreciate that by designing our institutions, we are also designing ourselves—the people who inhabit the institutions—at least in part. But this is a responsibility we must all accept. And the first step to taking responsibility over the structure of our workplace is to start asking questions. When it comes to the design of work, we must ask "Why?" What is the purpose of this work? Will the purpose of the work inspire people to do their jobs as Luke did his custodial job in the hospital? We must ask "What?" Is the product of our work something that will actually provide a benefit? Are the results of our transactions with customers positive sum, so that both sides leave the transaction better off? It will be much easier to inspire our workforce if the answer to this question is yes, even if we aren't saving lives or saving the earth, if we are making the lives of the people we serve at least a little bit better. And we must ask "How?" Are we giving workers the freedom to use their intelligence and discretion to help solve the problems they face every workday? Are we allowing them to work without close supervision, and trusting that since they want to do their jobs well, they will?

I'm focusing here on the structure of the work and the workplaces that people face because I think that there are real limits to what people can do as individuals in environments that are extremely inhospitable to doing work that is meaningful. But I don't want to let people off the hook entirely. Not every hospital custodian finds meaning in his or her work, but Luke and some of his colleagues did. They pulled this magic off by crafting their jobs, as Amy Wrzesniewski puts it, so that the jobs included more than the long list of menial tasks contained in the official job description. Often, if not always, people find themselves in work situations that allow them to find meaning and engagement, if they are willing to look for it. So even in unpromising situations, each of us, as individuals, can resist the ideology that tells us we don't really care what work is like as long as we're being well paid for it. We can demand of ourselves the effort to find the ways in which other people benefit if we do our jobs with enthusiasm rather than indifference.

The world of work, and thus the world of human experience, will be a very different place if we ask ourselves these questions about the work we do, and the work we ask others to do. And human nature will be different too. We will enable the people who work for us to live richer lives, and everyone will benefit.

The last question we need to ask is "When?" Are these troubled times the right occasion to try to change the work we do? Shouldn't we wait until the economy is more prosperous and more stable? There will always be excuses to stay with what is familiar. There will always be reasons to resist reshaping both our conception of work and our conception of human nature. But I don't think there are good reasons. Indeed, the transformation of work may contribute in significant ways to both the prosperity and the stability of our economic system. And even if it doesn't put more money in our pockets or more stuff in our houses, it will enrich our lives in ways that really matter.

The industrial revolution lifted millions of people in the Western world out of poverty. And now that it has spread to people and places that missed the first wave of industrialization, it is relieving the poverty of many millions more. Industrialization has been a spectacular human achievement. But as it has relieved material poverty, it has done so at the price of poverty of spirit. Perhaps this was a necessary price to pay at earlier stages of economic development. But that is no longer the case. When it comes to the transformation of the human workplace, there is really no time like the present.

In an interview with *Rolling Stone* magazine many years ago, rock superstar Bruce Springsteen said this about his own stunningly successful career:

> I understand that it's the music that keeps me alive. . . . That's my lifeblood. And to give that up for, like, the TV, the cars, the houses—that's not the American dream. That's the booby prize, in the end. Those are the booby prizes. And if you fall for them— if, when you achieve them, you believe that this is the end in and of itself—then you've been suckered in. Because those are the consolation prizes, if you're not careful, for selling yourself out, or letting the best of yourself slip away. So you gotta be vigilant. You gotta carry the idea you began with further. And you gotta hope that you're headed for higher ground.

We as a society shouldn't settle for the booby prize any longer. It is time for us to demand of ourselves and of the people we work for and with that they seek higher ground. Together we can expose the ideas about human nature that have for too long shaped the workplace as nothing but ideology. The result will be better doctors, lawyers, teachers, hairdressers, and janitors, and healthier patients, better-educated students, and more satisfied clients and customers. And each of us will have had a hand in creating a human nature that is worth living up to.

ACKNOWLEDGMENTS

I have been thinking about the ideas in this book for more than forty years. Though I came to Swarthmore College with a PhD and an excellent pedigree in experimental psychology, my education really began once I started teaching. Colleagues Richard Schuldenfrei and Hugh Lacey in philosophy, and Ken Sharpe in political science, helped me to see that what I thought of as a set of fairly narrow empirical problems in the discipline in which I was trained were actually broad and deep problems that spanned all of social science. I am grateful to them for their patience in educating me, and I am grateful to Swarthmore College for fostering an intellectual environment in which inter-disciplinary conversation and collaboration are encouraged and admired. Without these good friends and teachers, there would have been no book for me to write.

More recently, I have benefitted a great deal from collabo-ration with Amy Wrzesniewski and Adam Grant. As you have seen, Amy's work especially figured prominently in what pre-ceded. In addition, Amy read an early version of the book and prevented me from committing a few serious errors of omission.

I am deeply indebted to Chris Anderson, who has given me numerous opportunities to present my ideas at TED. When I gave my first TED Talk in 2005 I would never have dreamed that millions of people, from all over the world, would eventually see it. I gave my most recent TED Talk in 2013, and this book grew out of it. I thank June Cohen for giving me the opportunity, and Michelle Quint for providing insightful editorial suggestions.

I also want to thank Allison Dworkin for reading the first draft of the book and sharing with me her critical insights along with the encouragement to respond to them.

Finally, I want to thank Myrna Schwartz. Myrna and I have been partners in life for fifty years. There is not an idea in this book that we have not discussed repeatedly. For all our lives together, Myrna has been my touchstone and my sounding board. She has also been a model of what work can be when it is good.

WORKS CITED AND FURTHER READING

Note: Some of the references below are specific works mentioned in the text whereas others offer a somewhat broader perspective on what work is and what it can be. These more general works, some of which may also be mentioned in the text, have an asterisk [*] at the end of the citation.

Anderson, R. C. *Confessions of a Radical Industrialist: Profits, People, Purpose—Doing Business by Respecting the Earth*. New York: St. Martin's Press, 2009.

Barley, S. R., and G. Kunda. "Design and Devotion. Surges of Rational and Normative Ideologies of Control in Managerial Discourse." *Administrative Science Quarterly* (1992): 37, 363–99.

Bowles, S. "Policies Designed for Self-interested Citizens May Undermine 'the Moral Sentiments': Evidence from Economic Experiments." *Science* 320 (2008): 1605–609.*

Cohen, R. C., and R. I. Sutton. "Clients as a Source of Enjoyment on the Job: How Hairstylists Shape Demeanor and Personal Disclosures." In J. A. Wagner, III (ed.), *Advances in Qualitative Organization Research* (pp. 1–32). Greenwich, CT: JAI Press, 1998.*

Darling-Hammond, L. *The Right to Learn*. New York: Jossey-Bass, 1997.*

Deci, E. L. *Intrinsic Motivation*. New York: Plenum, 1975.*

Deci, E. L., and R. M. Ryan. *Intrinsic Motivation and Self-Determination in Human Behavior*. New York: Plenum, 1985.*

DeVoe, S. E., and J. Pfeffer. "When Time Is Money: The Effect of Hourly Payment on the Evaluation of Time." *Organizational Behavior and Human Decision Processes* 104 (2007): 1–13.

——— "When Is Happiness About How Much You Earn? The Effect of Hourly Payment on the Money-Happiness Connection." *Personality and Social Psychology Bulletin*, 35 (2009): 1602–18.

Dweck, C. S. *Mindset: The New Psychology of Success*. New York: Random House, 2006.*

Dweck, C. S., and E. L. Leggett. "A Social-Cognitive Approach to Motivation and Personality." *Psychological Review*, 95 (1988): 256–73.*

Fredrickson, B. *Positivity*. New York: MFJ Books, 2009.*

Frey, B. S., and F. Oberholzer-Gee. "The Cost of Price Incentives: An Empirical Analysis of Motivation Crowding Out." *American Economic Review*, 87 (1997): 746–55.

Gallup Organization (2013). *State of the Global Workplace*.

Gawande, A. "The Cost Conundrum." *The New Yorker*, June 1, 2009: 55–68.

Geertz, C. *The Interpretation of Cultures*. New York: Basic Books, 1973.*

Gergen, K. J. "Social Psychology as History." *Journal of Personality and Social Psychology*, 26 (1973): 309-20.*

Gneezy, U., and A. Rustichini. "A Fine Is a Price." *Journal of Legal Studies*, 29 (2000): 1-17.

Grant, A. M. "How Customers Can Rally Your Troops." *Harvard Business Review*, June 2011: 97-103.

———. *Give and Take*. New York: Viking, 2013.*

Grant, A. M., and D. A. Hofmann. "It's Not All About Me: Motivating Hand Hygiene Among Health Care Professionals by Focusing on Patients." *Psychological Science*, 11 (2011): 1494-99.*

Haidt, J. *The Righteous Mind: Why Good People Are Divided by Politics and Religion*. New York: Random House, 2012.*

Heath, C. "On the Social Psychology of Agency Relationships: Lay Theories of Motivation Overemphasize Extrinsic Incentives." *Organizational Behavior and Human Decision Processes*, 78 (1999): 25-62.

Heslin, P. A., G. P. Latham, and D. VandeWalle. "The Effect of Implicit Person Theory on Performance Appraisals." *Journal of Applied Psychology*, 90 (2005): 842-56.

———. "Keen to Help? Managers' Implicit Person Theories and Their Subsequent Employee Coaching." *Personnel Psychology*, 59 (2006): 871-902.

Heyman, J., and D. Ariely. "Effort for Payment: A Tale of Two Markets." *Psychological Science*, 15 (2004): 787-93.

Hilfiker, D. "A Doctor's View of Modern Medicine." *New York Times Magazine*, February 23, 1986: 44-47, 58.

Hirsch, F. *Social Limits to Growth*. Cambridge, MA: Harvard Press, 1976.*

Hodson, R. *Dignity at Work*. New York: Cambridge University Press, 2001.*

Judge, T. A., R. F. Piccolo, N. P. Podsakoff, J. C. Shaw, and B. L. Rich. "The Relationship Between Pay and Job Satisfaction: A Meta-Analysis of the Literature." *Journal of Vocational Behavior*, 77 (2010): 157-67.

Jussim, L. "Self-fulfilling Prophecies: A Theoretical and Integrative Review." *Psychological Review*, 93 (1986): 429-45.

———. "Teacher Expectations: Self-Fulfilling Prophecies, Perceptual Biases, and Accuracy." *Journal of Personality and Social Psychology*, 57 (1989): 469-80.

Jussim, L., J. Eccles, and S. Madon. "Social Perception, Social Stereotypes, and Teacher Expectations: Accuracy and the Quest for the Powerful Self-Fulfilling Prophecy." *Advances in Experimental Social Psychology*, 28 (1996): 281-388.

Keynes, J. M. *The General Theory of Employment, Interest, and Money* (originally published in 1936). New York: Harcourt, 1965.*

Kohn, A. *Punished by Rewards*. Boston: Houghton Mifflin, 1993.*

Kohn, M. L., and C. Schooler. "Job Conditions and Personality: A Longitudinal Assessment of Their Reciprocal Effects." *American Journal of Sociology*, 87 (1982): 1257–83.

Kronman, A. T. *The Lost Lawyer*. Cambridge, MA: Harvard University Press, 1993.*

Lepper, M. R., and D. Greene (eds.). *The Hidden Costs of Reward*. Hillsdale, New Jersey: Erlbaum, 1978.*

Lepper, M. R., D. Greene, and R. E. Nisbett. "Undermining Children's Intrinsic Interest with Extrinsic Rewards: A Test of the 'Overjustification Hypothesis.' " *Journal of Personality and Social Psychology*, 28 (1973): 129–37.

MacIntyre, A. *After Virtue*. South Bend, IN: University of Notre Dame Press, 1981.*

Madon, S., L. Jussim, and J. Eccles. "In Search of the Powerful Self-Fulfilling Prophecy." *Journal of Personality and Social Psychology*, 72 (1997): 791–809.

Marglin, S. A. "What Do Bosses Do?: The Origins and Functions of Hierarchy in Capitalist Production." *Review of Radical Political Economics*, 6 (1974): 60–112.*

McGregor, D. M. *The Human Side of Enterprise*. New York: McGraw-Hill, 1960.*

Merton, R. K. "The Self-Fulfilling Prophecy." *The Antioch Review*, 8 (1948): 193–210.*

Miller, D. T. "The Norm of Self-Interest." *American Psychologist*, 54 (1999): 1053–60.

Nisbett, R. E. *Intelligence and How to Get It: Why Schools and Cultures Count*. New York: Norton, 2009.*

Pfeffer, J. *The Human Equation*. Cambridge: Harvard Business Review Press, 1998.*

Pfeffer, J., and S. E. DeVoe. "Economic Evaluation: The Effect of Money and Economics on Time Use Attitudes." *Journal of Economic Psychology*, 30 (2009): 500–8.

Pink, D. *Drive: The Surprising Truth About What Motivates Us*. New York: Penguin, 2009.*

Rose, M. *The Mind at Work: Valuing the Intelligence of the American Worker*. New York: Viking, 2004.*

Rosenthal, R., and L. Jacobson. *Pygmalion in the Classroom: Teacher Expectation and Pupils' Intellectual Development*. New York: Holt, Rinehart & Winston, 1968.

Ross, L., and A. Ward. "Naive Realism in Everyday Life: Implications for Social Conflict and Misunderstanding." In T. Brown, E. S. Reed, and E. Turiel (eds.), *Values and Knowledge*: 103–35. Hillsdale, NJ: Erlbaum, 1996.

Ryan, R. M., and E. L. Deci. "Self-determination Theory and the Facilitation of Intrinsic Motivation, Social Development, and Well-being." *American Psychologist*, 55 (2000): 68–78.*

Schiltz, P. J. "On Being a Happy, Healthy, and Ethical Member of an Unhappy, Unhealthy, and Unethical Profession." *Vanderbilt Law Review*, 52 (1999): 871–918.

Schwartz, B. *The Battle for Human Nature*. New York: Norton, 1986.*

———. *The Costs of Living: How Market Freedom Erodes the Best Things in Life*. New York: Norton, 1994.*

———. "The Creation and Destruction of Value." *American Psychologist*, 45 (1990): 7–15.*

———. "Psychology, Idea Technology, and Ideology." *Psychological Science*, 8 (1997): 21–7.*

Schwartz, B., and K. Sharpe. *Practical Wisdom*. New York: Riverhead, 2010.*

Sen, A. "Rational Fools." *Philosophy and Public Affairs*, 6 (1976): 317–44.

Skinner, B. F. *Science and Human Behavior*. New York: Macmillan, 1953.*

Smith, A. *The Theory of Moral Sentiments* (originally published in 1753). Oxford: Clarendon Press, 1976.*

———. *The Wealth of Nations* (originally published in 1776). New York: Modern Library, 1937.*

Snyder, M., and E. D. Tanke. "Social Perception and Interpersonal Behavior: On the Self-Fulfilling Nature of Social Stereotypes." *Journal of Personality and Social Psychology*, 35 (1977): 655–66.

Sowell, T. *A Conflict of Visions*. New York: Morrow, 1987.*

Springsteen, B. Interview in *Rolling Stone*, December 6, 1984: 18–22, 70.

Stout, L. *Cultivating Conscience*. Princeton, NJ: Princeton University Press, 2011.*

Sullivan, W. M. *Work and Integrity*. New York: Jossey-Bass, 2004.*

Taylor, F. W. *The Principles of Scientific Management* (originally published in 1911). New York: Norton, 1967.

Wrzesniewski, A. "Caring in Constrained Contexts." Unpublished manuscript, 2009.*

———, and J. E. Dutton. "Crafting a Job: Revisioning Employees as Active Crafters of Their Work." *Academy of Management Review*, 26 (2001): 179–201.*

———, J. E. Dutton, and G. Debebe. "Interpersonal Sensemaking and the Meaning of Work." *Research in Organizational Behavior*, 25 (2003): 93–135.*

———, C. McCauley, P. Rozin, and B. Schwartz. "Jobs, Careers, and Callings: People's Relations to Their Work." *Journal of Research in Personality*, 31 (1997): 21–33.*

ABOUT THE AUTHOR

Barry Schwartz is a professor of psychology at Swarthmore College, in Pennsylvania. Schwartz has written ten books and more than 100 articles for professional journals. In 2004, Schwartz published *The Paradox of Choice: Why More Is Less*, which was named one of the top business books of the year by both *Business Week* and *Forbes* magazine, and has been translated into twenty-five languages. Since its publication, Schwartz has published articles on various aspects of its main thesis in sources as diverse as *The New York Times*, *The New York Times Magazine*, *The Chronicle of Higher Education*, *Parade*, *The Atlantic*, *USA Today*, *Advertising Age*, *Slate*, *Scientific American*, *The New Republic*, *Newsday*, *AARP Bulletin*, *Harvard Business Review*, and *The Guardian*. He spoke about it at the TED Conference in 2005, and has appeared on dozens of radio and TV shows, including NPR's *Morning Edition* and *Talk of the Nation*, *Anderson Cooper 360* (CNN), the *News Hour with Jim Lehrer* (PBS), *The Colbert Report*, and *CBS News Sunday Morning*. In 2009, Schwartz spoke at TED about our loss of wisdom. He subsequently published a book on this topic, *Practical Wisdom*, with his colleague Kenneth Sharpe.

Barry Schwartz's TED Talk, available for free at TED.com, is the companion to *Why We Work.*

Asa Mathat/TED

RELATED TALKS

Shawn Achor
The happy secret to better work
We believe that we should work to be happy, but could that be backward? In this fast-moving and entertaining talk, psychologist Shawn Achor argues that happiness actually inspires productivity.

Dan Pink
The puzzle of motivation
Career analyst Dan Pink examines the puzzle of motivation, starting with a fact that social scientists know but most managers don't: Traditional rewards aren't always as effective as we think. Listen for illuminating stories—and maybe, a way forward.

Tony Robbins
Why we do what we do
Tony Robbins discusses the "invisible forces" that motivate everyone's actions—and high-fives Al Gore in the front row.

Barry Schwartz
Our loss of wisdom
Barry Schwartz makes a passionate call for "practical wisdom" as an antidote to a society gone mad with bureaucracy. He argues powerfully that rules often fail us, incentives often backfire, and practical, everyday wisdom will help rebuild our world.

Beyond Measure:
The Big Impact of Small Changes
by Margaret Heffernan

In this wise and witty guide to creating strong company culture, business leader Margaret Heffernan lays the groundwork for a new kind of thinking: Organizations can create seismic shifts by making deceptively small changes.

Judge This
by Chip Kidd

Acclaimed book designer Chip Kidd explains the prime importance of first impressions, in design and life. In this playful, image-heavy, insight-rich book, Kidd explores the design of everyday objects, revealing the way design shapes our world, and offering fascinating lessons in first impressions that everyone can use.

ABOUT TED

TED is a nonprofit devoted to spreading ideas, usually in the form of short, powerful talks (eighteen minutes or less) but also through books, animation, radio programs, and events. TED began in 1984 as a conference where Technology, Entertainment, and Design converged, and today covers almost every topic—from science to business to global issues—in more than one hundred languages.

TED is a global community, welcoming people from every discipline and culture who seek a deeper understanding of the world. We believe passionately in the power of ideas to change attitudes, lives, and, ultimately, our future. On TED.com, we're building a clearinghouse of free knowledge from the world's most inspired thinkers—and a community of curious souls to engage with ideas and each other. Our annual flagship conference convenes thought leaders from all fields to exchange ideas.

Our TEDx program allows communities worldwide to host their own independent, local events, all year long. And our Open Translation Project ensures these ideas can move across borders.

In fact, everything we do—from the TED Radio Hour to the projects sparked by the TED Prize, from TEDx events to the TED-Ed lesson series — is driven by this goal: How can we best spread great ideas?

TED is owned by a nonprofit, nonpartisan foundation.

ABOUT TED BOOKS

TED Books are small books about big ideas. They're short enough to read in a single sitting, but long enough to delve deep into a topic. The wide-ranging series covers everything from architecture to business, space travel to love, and is perfect for anyone with a curious mind and an expansive love of learning. Each TED Book is paired with a related TED Talk, available online at TED.com. The books pick up where the talks leave off. An 18-minute speech can plant a seed or spark the imagination, but many talks create a need to go deeper, to learn more, to tell a longer story. TED Books fill this need.